I believe that a writer worth his salt at all has an obligation not only to entertain but to comment on the world in which he lives, not only to comment, but maybe have a shot at reshaping the world.
— ABBEY MANN, FILM WRITER/PRODUCER

I have given you authority to trample on snakes and scorpions and to overcome all the power of the enemy; nothing will harm you.
— LUKE 10:19

I recognize the badge of my office as a symbol of public faith, and I accept it as a public trust to be held so long as I am true to the ethics of the police service. I will constantly strive to achieve these objectives and ideals, dedicating myself before God to my chosen profession
...law enforcement.
— LAW ENFORCEMENT CODE OF ETHICS

FROM HELL TO HAIL MARY
A COP'S STORY

FROM HELL TO HAIL MARY
A COP'S STORY

BY FRANK DIPAOLA

October 2014

This book was written by Frank DiPaola and is based on his memory
of events, and of conversations with people from his past and from
the present. All names have been changed but events are real.
Any resemblance to any character and any living person is purely
coincidental. To the best of his knowledge, the information in this
book is true, within the margins of human memory.

FROM HELL TO HAIL MARY
A COP'S STORY

ISBN-13: 978-1500747039
ISBN-10: 1500747033

Printed in the United States

CONTENTS

PUBLISHER'S NOTE

At the time of this publication, police violence and the militarization of local police departments are garnering all too many headlines. Indeed, it may be auguring a sea change in how our nation is policed.

Those who are involved in seeking change to the way American streets are kept safe would be well advised to seek the advice of veterans of those streets, particularly people like Frank DiPaola, a man who put in his time serving and protecting the people of Los Angeles, competing with the gangs and drug dealers for the hearts and souls of children at risk.

As described in these pages, Frank's experience as a patrolman, doing dangerous undercover work, and in the LAPD Juvenile Impact Program – today having graduated 10,000 young men and women – could provide something of a road map for those seeking effective reform.

Ultimately, quality policing comes down to the hearts and minds of the men and women who come face to face with criminals and victims on a daily basis. Frank DiPaola, a man of intelligence, courage and faith, is the kind of person who would be successful in making any community safer, and more than that, in preventing crime by diverting criminals to a healthy and productive path before it is too late..

It is a privilege to publish Frank's book. Thanks to Michelle Manos Design for book design, Ed Greco for cover art, and John DiCarlo for proofreading.

Tony Seton
Carmel, California

FROM HELL TO HAIL MARY

DEDICATION

To my wife, Yara,
whose patience and tenacity kept me on point,
and the guidance of Mother Mary.

And to the many priests, cops, and kids whose friendship
and wisdom were truly inspirational.

To Captain Joe Curreri, Captain Keith Bushey, and
Officer Dominic Colenzo whose vision, leadership,
and hard work made the
L.A.P.D. Juvenile Impact Program
the success that it has become.

Special thanks to Father Emil for fine-tuning the title
of this book, and to Carlos, a man of great strength and
courage, who is like a son to me.

And thanks to my publisher, Tony Seton,
for putting up with me.

FROM HELL TO HAIL MARY

FOREWORD

MOST REVEREND RICHARD J. GARCIA, D.D.
Bishop of the Diocese of Monterey

(831) 373-4345
FAX: (831) 373-1175

RJG@dioceseofmonterey.org
www.dioceseofmonterey.org

January 15, 2015

Re: *From Hell to Hail Mary: A Cop's Story* by Frank Di Paola

At first glance the title of this book, written by Frank Di Paola, seems to be a paradox and to some maybe unbelievable. And yet it is, after deeper reflection, a magnificent portrayal for the reader of a human transformation and conversion in some ways similar to that of St. Paul the Apostle in the New Testament of the Bible.

I believe *From Hell to Hail Mary: A Cop's Story* is an invitation to witness the reality that only our God, with whom all things are possible, as St. Matthew tells us in his Gospel, can enable in one's life.

I also believe the reader will travel with the author on this journey of time and life changing experiences and thus be in awe of what is possible, if only we believe and hope for one another.

A blessed reading to you,

+Most Reverend Richard J. Garcia, D.D.
Bishop of the Diocese of Monterey

425 Church Street • P.O. Box 2048 • Monterey, California 93942-2048

FROM HELL TO HAIL MARY

INTRODUCTION

*Any man's death diminishes me, because I am involved in
mankind; and therefore never send to know for whom the bell tolls;
it tolls for thee. – JOHN DONNE*

I wrote this book because I had to. I needed to share what happened
with me as a cop in Los Angeles. How I did the roller coaster of crime and
punishment and wound up helping kids – some kids, anyway – turn away
from gangs and lead healthy lives.

It was a religious experience for me, literally; my faith gave me
my purpose. Things happened that were outside the realm of normal
understanding, but you don't have to believe in God to get what I'm talking
about. Like how I met my wife. Amazing. Wonderful. That's in here.

I also write about good politicians and cops – the good and the bad –
and about the City of Angels with tarnished wings, and the good that you
can find in almost everyone.

I believe that in the kingdom of God everyone has a mission, and this
book is about mine.

Frank DiPaola
September 2014

FROM HELL TO HAIL MARY

PREFACE

It was the tail end of the 70's. Jimmy Carter was trying to figure out what leadership meant. The country was lousy with cocaine, and disco and Donna Summer were all the rage. I traded the standard issue black-and-white Plymouth Fury, with the tin cans on top and the a/c that didn't work, for a sleek new ride that featured the Cadillac crest instead of the L.A. city seal. I was still "protecting and serving" but in stealth mode – cocktail straws and cocktails, bullshit and blow, out-cunning the cunning and conning the con. Welcome to my world.

I tooled the '78 silver-over-black Seville, a police freebie courtesy of Hertz – "We put you in the driver seat" – rent-a-car, through the garbage-strewn, rat maternity ward streets of L.A.'s decrepit skid row. A potpourri of dope fiends and beggars (who weren't homeless because they had spacious cardboard boxes to call home) eye-balled me and I back at 'em. An assorted array of gutter-sluts cruised the streets selling face time for five dollars or an around-the-world for a ten spot.

In today's world, the price of flesh has gone up – just like other commodities.

They wondered, "Was the white dude with the "fro" and the Serpico beard their next trick, their main man to a 30-minute euphoric trip to nowhere, or was he a cop?"

The third choice was the home run. I carried a badge, the same one Jack Webb made famous, only it wasn't badge number 714. It was badge number 7353. I carried it alongside a .38 caliber wheel-gun (that's a revolver) to compliment its oval symbol of truth and justice. I was a "tough tawkin' " dope cop in the City of Angels.

FROM HELL TO HAIL MARY

DOPE COPS -"TAWKIN' THE TAWK"

The devil deals from a deck full of aces; you have everything
and you have nothing. – FRANK DIPAOLA

August 1978. Early evening, I was making my way to the newly-completed LAPD central facilities building, a bunker-like, windowless fortress in the heart of skid row. Donna Summer came along for the ride, beckoning me to join her for a last dance. I wish. I would much rather have been heading to a bar on Sunset for a Jack on the rocks with a disco doll than driving through this dump.

L.A.'s skid row is like any other except worse. As darkness descends, trash can fires flame up, illuminating the gaunt, ghost-like figures that prowl the streets looking for their next prey or their next fix, which ever comes first. It was like driving through part of the movie set for the foreboding futuristic flick "Blade Runner."

The Fort housed Metro, SWAT, and Administrative Narcotics. It was also home to Central Division, the precinct that was supposed to keep the low-life's that called its streets home from crossing Broadway, an unofficial "magic line." It was meant to separate the civilized from the barbarians. Like a lot of "supposed-to's," it didn't work out that way.

I worked on the third floor, in the Administrative Narcotics Division, or "ad-narc" as it was called. Ad-narc cops work in a surreal atmosphere: half make-believe and half hardcore detective work. One of the highs that comes from working dope is the excitement of the unknown – the stomach-churning anxiety of reeling in a dealer while playing a character and the adrenalin rush from "booting a door" (kicking it down) without knowing what ominous threat waits on the other side. This was my home...at least for now.

The ad-narc squad room had a public phone booth with a red light on top (a la Get Smart) in the middle of the office. It was the hotline to the dozen-or-so dope cops and "UCs" (undercover guys) that manned ad-narc back in the day before cell phones and pagers. Large post-its with the aliases used by the dope cops next to their real names covered the inside of the booth. When a call came in, whoever was closest to the phone would pick up the receiver and greet the dope dealer or snitch with a cocky, smart-ass "Yeah?"

As I entered the bustling squad room, the red light on top of the booth was on. A gruff, bearded biker dope cop yelled out, "Hey Apollo, it's a live one." Apollo: that's me. When a cop goes "under," a new identity is established with a paper trail to match. I assumed the name "Frankie Apollo" from the character "Johnny Apollo," the suave and debonair tough guy immortalized in the 1940 movie of the same name.

The film noir Hollywood gangster movies were a trip. When not personally playing cops and robbers they provided the entertainment. One lucky evening I met George Raft while having dinner with my grandmother at Mateo's, a classy throw-back Italian joint on Westwood Boulevard frequented by the old Hollywood legends. I approached him and asked if he would say 'hello' to my grandmother, and he was more than happy to oblige. He took her by the hand, bowed, and respectfully greeted her. Hollywood stars had class in those days.

Before being able to play with the big boys in ad-narc, I had to do my time in "the bucket," as we called working low-life dope fiends and street slime in Hollywood. Detective-sergeant Bernard Katz (Uncle Bernie) recruited me out of Hollywood dope. I made my bones there because of my reputation as an operator with a strong "New Yawk" vibe with an obnoxiously gregarious demeanor.

As he good-naturedly said when he approached me, "You can take the boy out of Brooklyn, but you can't take the Brooklyn out of the boy."

Uncle Bernie figured I was a natural to operate the high-end clubs in Hollywood and Beverly Hills, sniffing my way up the white powder trail to mid- and high-end "coke" dealers who seldom got popped. Uncle Bernie made it quite clear that the term "sniff" was hyperbole. Smoking a little weed to further the investigation was okay, so long as it was disclosed in the reports, but anything else was a big "no-no." Finger-tasting the white powder is Hollywood cop drama, not reality.

Uncle Bernie looked more like a rabbi or an accountant than a cop. He was a real "corker," which is down-home Brooklyn for a "character." Uncle Bernie was a master of surveillance, and his rabbi routine was second to none. He could park himself on a drug dealer's front lawn and they wouldn't be wise. When it came to the art of interrogation, Uncle Bernie could make a suspect give it up before they realized they gave it up, and then thank him for helping them give it up.

Uncle Bernie also had a great sense of humor. One of my "CI's" (police lingo for 'confidential informant') gave it to me straight up that a messenger service in Century City was a front for a cocaine distribution network. I secured a search warrant, and under Uncle Bernie's rabbinical leadership, we took the place down. All the employees and occupants of the tenth floor luxury office were handcuffed, and a uniform officer was placed at the front door. Sol, the owner, was a sixty-something balding escapee from Brooklyn's Pitkin Avenue. He had a pudgy girth that lapped his white belt, was very Jewish, and very upset.

"How could the cops do such a thing?" he wailed. "My business, my business; you can't come in here like Gestapo!"

Uncle Bernie calmed him down. He took off the cuffs, and they started kibitzing like two yentas at a bagel shop on Fairfax. When we hit the place, there was a gorgeous blonde fox in the reception area. Turns out she was just answering an ad for a receptionist that Sol had placed. She would definitely be a big-time addition to the office decor, and help ease the daily stress of merging a legitimate messenger service with cocaine trafficking. She might even add a few follicles to Sol's balding cranium. While Bernie bonded with Sol, the rest of the squad painstakingly took the place apart. Suddenly, the relative calm was shattered by an obnoxious raspy voice that had seen too much nicotine in its day. Enter Mrs. Sol, battle-axe extraordinaire.

"Where is my husband?" "What are the police doing here?" "What the hell is going on?" Mrs. Sol blew by the uniformed cop in a whirlwind of ferocity, a Florida hurricane barreling over a palm tree. The drama became even more bellicose when she feasted her eyes on the mini-skirted blonde sitting in her husband's chair in hand-cuffs. She glared at Sol, who was sweating profusely.

"Who is she, Sol?" she barked.

Sol looked more terrified of his beloved bride from hell than of the police. She then turned on Uncle Bernie indignantly, "And who the hell are you?"

In true Inspector Clouseau fashion, Bernie replied "Sergeant Bernard Katz, LAPD vice. We're here conducting a call-girl investigation." He glanced over at the blonde. We all broke out in raucous laughter, but the wife from hell didn't see it that way. She went over to her poor helpless husband and smacked him so hard that the flesh-on-flesh sound cracked like an old time barber strap being struck by a straight razor.

"You two-timing latka," she wailed. (More about Uncle Bernie later.)

* * * * *

My undercover persona was Frankie Apollo. I was to be a New York hustler complete with gold chains, paisley shirt, and a "fro" that would do "Super Fly" proud. I modeled Frankie Apollo after some mob-connected types I had met growing up in New York. LAPD gave me bogus New York license plates for my Porsche 911 which I drove when I wasn't using a luxury rental ride to consummate a scam.

Getting paid to be a barfly in L.A.'s high end joints like Carlos 'n Charlie's, Pips, the Ginger Man, Alice's Restaurant, and assorted other tony purveyors of booze and broads. Sipping vodka and scoring dope from unsuspecting hustlers and players was definitely my idea of being on the clock. I loved L.A.!

After only a few weeks, this high-roller gig started to pay off. The blinking red light atop the phone booth signaled the call I had anxiously awaited. At the other end of the line was a Jamaican weasel named Dante Dinglebad. I picked up the receiver and responded coolly, "Yeah?"

"This Dante," he said in a pretentious tough-guy Jamaican pitch. I was tempted to say, "What's the dope?" Talking to a bad guy with "bad" as part of his name was corny enough. This telephone call was the alpha and the omega of something big. I had been trying to get this particular fish on the hook for four weeks. Now, he was biting.

Dante was big-time sleaze. He was the "go-to" guy at Carlos 'n Charlie's and some of the other clubs on the strip for those young and not-so-professional urban types who drove Beamers and Benzes and sipped Courvoisier. Carlos 'n Charlie's was on the corner of Sunset and Crescent Heights. The bar was usually heavy with T & A action in short skirts with slits that showed a lot of leg. Smoking, self-promoting banter and phony laughter filled the air. A couple of grams and a cheap cocktail straw were always handy if you wanted to get lucky with a party doll. The bottom line was "nobody wanted to go home alone," at least not without a buzz.

It was my first time out as Frankie Apollo, and Nick the bartender was as good as anybody to cozy up to and check out the white powder prospects. As I sipped the last of my second Black Russians (beer and straight bourbon were to be avoided, because that's what cops drank), I was about to get lucky. The sista that parked herself next to me at the bar had flawless ebony skin, two shades lighter than the black leather mini skirt that hugged her hips and thighs like O.J.'s gloves (more on O.J. later). She told me her name was Brenda. After the usual small talk and flirtatious repartee, my next line read something like, "How do you occupy yourself when you're not nursing Courvoisier's and charming wise guys from New York?"

"Are you a wise guy?"

"I'm a guy and I'm wise, so maybe the shoe fits," I answered. Brenda moistened her lower lip with her tongue and shifted her brown eyes from her cognac to me.

"I like to get high, and I like to make love."

"Let's start with the first and work our way to the second," I answered wistfully. I told her I had a chick in my apartment in the Marina who was expecting me back before midnight with enough blow to fill her empty mirror with a few lines to make us both happy before bedtime. I broke off with, "But tomorrow is another day."

Brenda slid her curvaceous tail off the stool, put her finger to my lips and said, "I can hook you up." She made her way to the pay phone on two gorgeous legs attached to a pair of sexy sable stilettos and returned a few minutes later wearing that "I got you handled" look. "My old man is on his way over. Dante is like Santa Claus around here, he'll take care of you."

"Does he take care of you too?"

"When I want him to, but I call my own shots."

A quick thirty minutes later the aforementioned Santa cruised in and cozied up to the bar. Instead of a white beard he had a white Stacy Adams suit that was trying to be linen, but was more like a 50/50 poly/rayon blend. His snakeskin loafers and gold chains complemented the ensemble; kudos to his haberdasher. I was impressed. Dante eyed me suspiciously, and Brenda made with the introductions. She told him that I was Italian, more specifically Sicilian, and called New York City home. The last name that followed Dante was Dinglebad. I gave him that "you've got to be kidding look" which coupled with Brenda's obvious carnal interest in me, didn't exactly make for terms of endearment between Santa Claus and me.

"I hear you're the golden goose laying the white eggs?" I sarcastically asked.

Dante took a sip of Brenda's drink, subliminally asserting his possession of Brenda as his main squeeze, and said, "Follow me." I followed him and his white suit into the men's room. Dante looked like the Devil. He was darker then Brenda, with a thin, skull-like face that came to a point in a narrow daggerish mandible, his pointed ears framing his face like book ends. Very cool, I thought – ebony and ivory housing the soul of evil. Very cool pal.

After checking out the stalls to make sure we were alone, Dante proceeded to set me wise. "Brenda says you cool. I don't normally deal this quick, and I like to know my customers first. So what you need?"

"How much a gram?" I asked.

He gave me a narrow-lipped smile and in a bitingly sarcastic tone came at me with, "Shit, mon, you get me down here for pigeon droppings. I think you want serious quantity!"

"I wanna check out your stuff make sure it's not bunk. A gram first, and if it's good, we'll talk. How much?"

"A buck and a half."

"Too much, try again," I snapped. (One of the biggest mistakes a dope cop can make is to jump at the dealer's first price in his zeal to make the buy. It's like going to Tijuana; you're expected to bargain.)

As per Uncle Bernie's tutelage, "When they blurt out a price, that's just a starting point. Make believe it's your own money, and not the department's." We were bobbing and weaving now, and I had to play all the angles.

Dante thought it over, rolled his eyes and said, "Okay mon, one hundred twenty-five large, dat's it for now, best I can do."

He reached into the side pocket of the tablecloth suit and handed me a small plastic baggy of white powder. I looked around and handed him some green with Ben Franklin's and Andrew Jackson's mugs. Santa Claus made with that narrow sinister smile again and began to set me wise: Brenda wasn't up for grabs, and that if I were a cop and not straight up with him, his posse would take care of my longevity.

I set him even wiser. "Listen brother and perk those pointed ears of yours up so they don't miss anything. I'm Sicilian, I'm from New York, and I have a family too, a big one. I wasn't born into it but I spilled blood, so put two and two together and see what you come up with! Now maybe you can deliver or maybe you can't, but if you can keep me in pocket with some quantity, my uncle and cousins back on the block will be very happy. You might even have business partner potential, so this shit better be real fine and not be big-time stepped on."

I stared him down like a matador in a bull ring. My man Dante got the picture. As I learned from an old savvy "closer" named Vinny, whom I worked with as a salesman at an Oldsmobile dealer in Queens, "After the spoken word and the stare-down eyeball conversation, he who speaks first loses."

Dante spoke first, "Who you connected to?" His tone was now more inquisitive than menacing.

I answered, "Just like poker, Dante, you never spill the hand until its right. Oh, and about the broad...friendly conversation baby, it ain't nothing."

I turned slowly and left Dante behind with the urinals. He knew I was no chump. We had established the parameters of our relationship like a couple of pack dogs. Respect is based on love or fear. In the underworld and police work it is usually the latter.

* * * * *

Once when I was working Hollywood dope, I had been kicking it with two gypsies. They were part of a swarm crammed into a post WWII era bungalow on Fountain just off Vine. It was only a few blocks from the infamous Hollywood and Vine, but it was a million miles and a million years from the glory of its heyday. The gypsies hooked me up with a Rastafarian (I'll call him Rasty, for short) who supplied local school kids with their daily dose of weed, hash, and sensimilla (the really good smoke). For the Rasty, marijuana was a path to God. For the kids, it was a path to nowhere. We were in his apartment, in the process of consummating a buy, when Rasty gets real nervous halfway through his second joint. He doesn't just look at me.

He looks right through me. "I get bad vibes from you, mon, like maybe you're a cop".

"Frankie's no cop, he's good people," gypsy number 1 offers up in my defense. Gypsy number two's stupor could only add a lethargic, cannabis-induced, "Yeah."

In undercover work, as in sports, the best defense is a good offense. I went into maniac mode. Bad guys are no different than the rest of us when it comes to dealing with violent psychos. They want to put distance between them and the nut job. To throw Rasty completely off the track, I jumped up and grabbed him by his collar and starting spitting (literally) profane venom. My movements were quick, jerky, and spastic, like a character out of One Flew Over the Cuckoo's Nest. "I ain't no fucking cop. Don't ever call me that again, scum bag!"

Rasty immediately started wiping the spit I had showered over his fear-stricken face. "You are crazy, mon." He turned to the gypsies, "Get him the fuck away from me, he's disgusting."

I yelled at him, "Do we do the deal or not?"

"Okay, okay," he yelled back, trying to calm me down.

The fear factor had kicked in.

Rasty threw several bags of weed on the table and in a near panic blurted out, "Just leave, mon, just leave."

I stared straight at him, wild-eyed, letting some drool from my lower lip drip down my chin to enhance his already psycho impression of me. I tossed the money at his feet. When the deal was done, I walked to the front door to signal my two partners to come in and make the bust. We always carried a lead-filled battering ram in the trunk of our plain-wrapped Plymouth, but if I could keep the door open long enough we wouldn't have to use it.

When Rasty saw two white guys with long hair exiting the Plymouth with the baby hub caps and no white walls, he knew he had been had. He positioned his tall wiry frame behind the door and tried to push me out. I body slammed the door (with him behind it) into the wall. Unfortunately for him, his nose got in the way and it split open like a watermelon at a Sunday barbecue. Torrents of blood rushed out of his partially smashed face. His angry eyes shot back at me like cannon balls. Since I didn't have any cuffs, I had to wedge myself behind him and choke him out. In the heat of battle, Rasty's blood got all over me.

When my partners finally threw themselves through the doorway and saw the crimson chaos, Detective Joe bellowed, "Frank's been hurt!" Before I could explain that the blood wasn't mine fists went flying. The fight was on.

Later, when I was booking Rasty, I asked him, "So what did you learn from all of this, pal?"

"Nothing. You fucked me."

"No, the lesson is always go with your gut instinct."

* * * * *

Okay, back to Dante Dinglebad and beautiful Brenda, the ebony temptress. For the next four to five weeks, we were the happy threesome, and when one of Brenda's girlfriends was around, a foursome. The word got out (how, I can't imagine) that I was "connected" and my Porsche 911 with the New York plates and the translucent copper paint job was the darling of the Sunset Boulevard valets. I always threw plenty of green around which added to my glitzy mystique. Good old Dante though, he never quite knew how to read me. I did my best to keep him off guard. When toking up at a party, Dante would watch me finesse a joint. I did my best not to inhale. It wasn't a Bill Clinton thing; I just couldn't stand the stuff, and it burned my throat. Also, a booze and cannabis cocktail doesn't exactly help in the "let's keep a clear head department."

"White boys don't know how to smoke, just like they don't know how to dance," Dante jokingly snorted. Brenda took the joint and proceeded to educate me salaciously on the finer points of getting high, Brenda style.

After numerous small-time buys of weed, coke, and you-name-it, Uncle Bernie decided that it was time for Dante to go to jail. I set up a four-ounce coke buy, but before Dante would go through with it, I had to agree to meet him at my apartment in Marina Del Rey, so he could check me out and make sure I was who I was supposed to be.

The Oakwood Garden apartments off Via Marina provided the perfect cover. A good friend of mine was the manager, and she could make a furnished apartment available on a moment's notice, complete with full and spent booze bottles and some women's lingerie so I could live up to my reputation. On this particular day, the sun hung low in the Marina, and the traffic on the 405 was thick – so thick that I was running late for Dante's scheduled visit. No big, I figured, since dope dealers are always fashionably late. It's part of their m.o.

As I pulled into the parking lot, I noticed Dante's Jag. You couldn't miss it, because the stock grill had been replaced with a triple thick, gold-plated aftermarket type. If grills could talk, this one would have screamed out, "I gotta be somebody." Since he was obviously waiting in the lobby area, I didn't want to walk into the front door or it might look like I didn't live here. I had to switch to Plan B. I swung the 911 back on to Via Marina and pulled into the underground parking lot. I parked and bolted into the elevator to the third floor, got out, and took the stairs to the lobby. The big "D" was pacing back and forth constantly glancing at his phony gold Rolex.

"My man, my man," I yelled, "You're late."

"Don't do me that way, I been here fifteen minutes. The lady here at the desk say you don't answer."

"Dante, there are some things in life that are even more important than you baby, and now that she's gone, we can take care of business."

The apartment looked great. The bed was in disarray, and on the night stand, there was an empty bottle of D.P. (Dom Perignon) and two champagne glasses, one smudged around the rim with freshly applied "I love you so much" red lipstick.

Dante looked nervous, "We got to do this thing tomorrow, mon."

"Whatever you say, Dante." (Inside I'm thinking, "I hope nobody else in the squad has a caper going tomorrow.") "Where and when?"

"I'll call you tomorrow, mon, let you know." It's an unwritten rule of dope dealers not to give out a location until the last minute, just in case there is a rip-off or the cops are in on it.

"Don't you even want a drink before you leave? It'll calm your nerves."

"No, mon, no. I don't want to get stopped by the police or nothing."

I took a circuitous route back to the station, using Venice Boulevard and surface streets just in case Dante or one of his dope fiend friends was running counter surveillance on me. My head was on a swivel. When you work undercover, you have to grow eyes in the back of your head – and on both sides. I gunned the 911 hard in and out of traffic so that a tail would be obvious. If this deal happened, it would be the biggest hand-to-hand buy the squad ever had.

"Fly, Robin, Fly" traveled into my airspace from the Blaupunkt and echoed my mood. I was flying high with angst. I decided to stop at the Mexican Village on Sunset Boulevard, where Frankie Apollo wasn't known, for a couple of tequila shooters. The shooters would be my pre-bust celebration and calm the nerves that were starting to jitter in anticipation. Was I nervous because Dante was nervous? Or was I worried that he would rip me off? Anxious thoughts danced in my brain. Maybe Dante had made me after all, and the joke was on me. The third shooter finally took the edge off. Tomorrow was another day; a big one.

It was eleven o'clock the next day when the phone booth light flashed crimson and the biker dope cop yelled out, "Hey Apollo. You've got a live one."

I was excited and scared. Only this time, Jose Cuervo wasn't around to dull my antsy nerves. I grabbed the phone, "Yeah?"

"Frankie this Dante, two o'clock at Pasadena Mall. Pull into the Colorado entrance to the lot. I be in my Jag. You see me at the entrance and we hook up. What ride you gonna have, the Seville or the 911?"

"The Seville, see ya at two." I was worried that there might be gun play, and there was no way I was letting the bronze beauty from Stuttgart stop lead.

Uncle Bernie hastily assembled the squad. We only had two hours to show time. Two point-men and half a dozen detectives had to be deployed to the location; air support had to be notified for a fly-by, and the Pasadena police department had to be informed so that backup units would be requested to stand by. During the briefing Uncle Bernie took control in his laid back but authoritative fashion.

"Now, Frankie-boy, have the suspect get in your car. When he flashes the dope, tell him you have to get the money out of the trunk. When the trunk is open that'll be the signal that the deal is a go, and we'll pounce. Whatever you do, don't split anywhere with him."

"Got it boss."

I watched in anticipation as the squad donned their bulletproof vests and LAPD-emblazoned navy blue raid jackets while also checking their heat. As I pulled the Seville past the guard shack and exited onto Sixth, I was oblivious to the neglected characters that adorned the dilapidated landscape. They were no longer of any interest to me. My focus was on Dante and that sinister face of his. Then it dawned on me. "Dante's Inferno." The book was about hell. Was Dante the devil? Was I driving into hell?

It was raining. The windshield wipers pulsated and banged against the windshield frame as though they were sounding the war drums. The throbbing beat of "Born to be Alive" and the words "to be alive, to be alive…" echoed eerily from the Delco sound box. It was as if the singer was trying to warn me. This cacophony of background noise added to my anxiety. I killed the radio, but it didn't help. More negativity started bombarding my brain. What if this was a rip? What if I screwed up? A thousand what-if's closed in on me. I reached into my pocket and grabbed hold of the Miraculous Medal of the Virgin Mary. I'd carried it since my days as a kid at St. Boniface and let go of a quick Hail Mary. "Hail Mary full of grace. The Lord is with thee. Blessed art thou amongst women . . . ." Time stood still. A calming presence descended. She soothed me like a cool shower on a humid day. I put away the medal and checked to make sure my two-inch .38 was still hugging my ankle. The devil and demons were ready to be met.

I pulled into the cavernous parking structure, studied my rear view mirror, and scanned the lot for the secretly deployed squad. I saw no one. Either their stealth mode was real good, or they'd all gotten lost. I was purposely late again, not wanting to tip my hand by seeming overzealous.

Dante, the dope man, was standing next to the tricked-out remains of a once noble

Jaguar, chewing up the final half inch of his Benson & Hedges. He looked around nervously like an expectant whore waiting for her next trick. He wore the same Stacy Adams tablecloth suit he'd been wearing the night we first met. As I pulled up, Dante abruptly discarded his cigarette, which still had a lot of mileage left. He opened the Seville's passenger door and threw himself into the stitched Corinthian leather.

"You in pocket?" I asked.

Dante responded nervously, "Well yeah, not exactly. We got to drive up to the third level." He was going a mile a minute.

"Where's the dope?"

"We got to drive upstairs, mon, my partner got it."

I jumped all over him.

"The deal was for you to come alone. This better not be a rip off or you go back to Jamaica in a box!" I bridled in a rage. "Your main man wouldn't front you that much quantity, would he? That's it isn't it?"

"Yeah, you right." he reluctantly admitted.

"You fucking lightweight."

"He wants you to come up to the third floor, the dope's up top in another ride."

My mind raced in all different directions at once. I felt like I was on a merry-go-round, going around and around but getting nowhere. I had to get off but it was spinning too fast to jump.

"Trust me Frankie, everything be cool."

Dante was a guy you could trust all right, to shoot you in the gut when you turned your head for a split second. Uncle Bernie's last words resonated in my brain, "Stick to the plan and don't split." I had about ten seconds to decide what to do.

I had invested too much into this thing to blow it now. Dante's change of plans put my cerebral cortex on overload.

Dante added, "My main man do it this way to make sure you not the cops."

"You guys have been watching too much television, this ain't the French Connection. You go upstairs and get the dope and I'll wait here. You can bring your main man down to me and do the deal like we said."

"No good mon, Alexander set it up. It got to go down his way, or no deal."

I got in the Jag with Dante. It was a crucial call, but sense number six told me it was the way to go. I had a great deal of self-confidence and even if things went sideways, I figured I could get Dante and company before they got me. I knew the wrath of Uncle Bernie would come down on me like an avalanche, but so be it.

"I'll go up with you but the money stays here. If this is a rip-off, you guys come up dry."

Dante came back at me, "Where's it at?"

"When I see the blow you'll find out. Maybe I played musical cars, too."

Dante's Jag with the two opposing players wound its way up the parking garage. Who would check mate who? I imagined Uncle Bernie screaming into the mic, "What the hell is he doing?" and the squad frantically running up the stairs, sweating profusely with each step, trying to keep the Jag in sight. It must have been ninety degrees in there.

After what seemed like an eternity, we reached the top and pulled up next to a red 350 SL with the top down. It was empty. Dante slithered out from under his steering wheel like the snake he was, and I followed.

He unlocked the trunk of the convertible, pointed to a brown satchel and said, "Have a look."

I did. It was filled with white gold. Out of the corner of my eye, I noticed a male black in a white Mercedes. He was watching. That must be Alexander, his main man.

Dante and I got back into the Jag and headed down. The white Mercedes followed. I held onto the satchel like it was the Maltese Falcon. There were cars everywhere – it must have been discount day at The Broadway. It seemed like forever before we got down to the first level and the point of no return. We cruised up behind the Seville, blocking it in the stall. I jumped out with the stash.

"Wait here, I'll go get the green."

I'm thinking to myself about three minutes to show time, but I was afraid Alexander would get away in the confusion. About ten seconds later, unmarked cars and unmarked cops descended on us like a torrential rain from a cloud burst. With too many guns pointed at his head, Dante's Jamaican jaw went into a nose dive.

"That guy Frank. He's got the dope!"

I pulled my .38 two inch from it's home next to my ankle and pointed it at Dante's diabolical head. "No man, you're the dope."

I didn't know if Dante was going to suck wind or throw up. Any remnants of his composed coolness were gone in sixty seconds. In the meantime, Alexander gunned the Benz in flight, but was bumper-smashed in place by Uncle Bernie and company.

Dante's eyes flashed at me and in a tone that came from the bowels of his gut said, "You're a cop? Mon, I've been had?"

Check mate. I was elated. Not only did we make the buy, but we even got Dante's supplier, two for the price of one. I still had to face Uncle Bernie.

He ambled up to me, "Good work kid, but you're fired."

Uncle Bernie was a man of few words. With a look of disappointment at what he felt he had to do, he said, "We'll talk later."

The next day, Uncle Bernie took me out to the wood shed. It went something like this: "You're a real good player kid, but you're a loose cannon. You not only take this job right to the end of the line, but you cross it. There are boundaries in police work, but your obsession with the mission makes them invisible to you. Sooner or later, you're going to get yourself killed or in a jam. I'm too old for this shit."

He gave me a month to wrap up my other investigations before I would be returned to uniform as a beat cop in Hollywood. Great. After all this, it looked like answering radio calls and writing traffic tickets would be my destiny. This was not the long good-bye, though. I'll be back.

THE NOT-SO-LONG GOOD-BYE
Death's kingdom is his life, he called for the soul to descend and
but alone, walk blithely through lost bliss.
— FROM *DANTE'S INFERNO*

From the ridiculous to the sublime: the past was telling to the future. Two days short of losing my locks at the local barber shop a fortuitous and funny thing happened. I got a call from Hollywood dope. They wanted me back. My old partner Detective Sergeant Amos Ridley must have rung the lieutenant's bell and put the fix in. I was to start Monday. My solemn bummer look beamed happy. I knew I'd be back eventually, but I didn't think it would happen this soon.

Amos was a black cop I had partnered up with from time to time in the past, and he was a hell of an operator. He could shuck and jive with the brothers and lay it on thicker than maple syrup. Amos was more "hook 'em and book 'em" oriented than an administrative type, but after the Dante dope man caper, he caringly suggested that we better play it pretty close to the double-yellow.

Amos always wore an olive drab army field jacket and black t-shirt underneath with some gold bling to accentuate the ensemble. It was the perfect undercover wear. You could operate two-bit street fiends by day, but it also worked for the club scene at night. To go along with my Brooklyn persona, a black leather jacket and an open shirt worked just fine. Amos looked mean with his full blown 1970's Afro and Fu Manchu, but his insides were pure gold with a heart bigger than a blown-up balloon on Valentine's Day. We would engage in witty banter about my paddy 'fro being kinkier and fuller than his. His comment was always the same: "You looking good for a white boy, but that's where it ends, my brotha." We shared a good laugh and then went about taking care of arresting business.

In between follow-ups we would work on anonymous clues phoned in to the 800 "we-tip" line. One of those clues involved a high-priced call girl dealing cocaine out of her plush penthouse pad on Franklin near La Brea. After a long elevator ride to the heights of penthouse heaven we finally arrived. Amos rang the buzzer of the mahogany apartment door. As most of the other apartment doors were painted a flat boring color, hers set the tone of what the interior offered.

The door opened just far enough as the gold security chain would allow. Greeting us were a pair of green metallic eyes attached to a dark complexioned brunette who had obviously spent more time at the beach and the pool than behind a typewriter in an office somewhere. Amos spoke first before the inquiring pair of enticing lips could speak.

"LAPD. We're conducting a narcotics investigation, may we come in?" We flashed our badges.

"If you guys are trick-or-treating you're either a few months too early or too late, but sure, come on in," she replied.

The place was pure class and so was she, even without make-up.

"I'm Nicole. Do you have ID cards to go with those badges? Not that I don't trust you, but a girl can't be too careful, you know?" she said with a smile. Convinced that we were the real deal, she started to laugh.

"Are you guys sure you're not vice?"

"No, narcotics," I said.

Amos explained that she was the subject of an anonymous tip, that we didn't have a search warrant, and would like her permission for a consent cursory search. If we didn't find dope, we would be on our merry way.

The Santa Ana's winds were blowing warm air that day, and the strong aroma of her Charlie cologne circulated throughout the upscale apartment, thanks to the open sliding glass door. She asked our first names.

"Frank and Amos," I responded in my best matter of fact "Dragnet" tone.

"You guys sure don't look like cops", she said coyly.

"That's the whole idea," I responded. Amos and I conducted as thorough a search as possible without being too intrusive. While she waited, she walked out on the balcony to have a smoke, eying us suspiciously.

After ten minutes of finding nothing except enough lingerie to fill a Frederick's of Hollywood catalogue, and some nude glossies of Nicole in various stages of undress, I was convinced that the anonymous tipper was probably a disgruntled trick or pissed-off competitor. We were ready to call it a day. Amos was finishing up in the kitchen and Nicole and I were making small talk about her photo album and trick clientele. Amos then pulled a bottle from the refrigerator filled with a semi-thick liquidly substance. He asked me if I had ever seen dope that looked like this.

Before I could answer, Nicole said, "Those are trophies from my tricks, bottled testimony of sexual satisfaction," she proudly explained.

Amos almost dropped the bottle in disgusted disbelief.

Nicole then tried to switch the mood from the depraved back to the seductive and added, "I would love to do a three-some in black-'n-white, and just like coffee at Winchell's Doughnuts, boys. It's on the house for the police."

I didn't know whether to laugh or throw up. Amos and I looked at each other; he immediately made a mad dash for the kitchen sink where he scrubbed his hands.

When he thought he was germ free, he said in a huff, "We're out of here. Thanks Nicole. We're both flattered, but we don't need to be part of anybody's sperm bank."

We had two more people to deprive of their freedom before going end of watch. Our next visit was to a small-time dope dealer named Mario, who called the second-floor apartment in a once elegant art deco structure from the Thirties on Argyle Street his home. I had made several "buys" from Mario in the last few weeks, and now his time had come. Mario opened the door with joint in hand. I introduced Amos, and Mario eyed him suspiciously.

"He's good people. Not to worry," I assured him.

Mario offered us a joint as a matter of cordial hospitality, and we both politely declined. He was watching TV, and Al Pacino, as Frank Serpico, filled the screen. Mario took a long hard look at Al Pacino's mug on the tube and than back at me.

"You look just like him, and your name is Frank too. How do I know you're not a cop?" I thought to myself I can't belief Al Pacino is going to screw up my hard-earned bust.

"Just ask me," I replied with a smile.

"Okay I will. Just for the record and to make it official, are you guys police officers?" (Bad guys always believe that if they ask, you must tell the truth, but not them).

"No," Amos and I answered in unison.

"Okay good, I'll go get the stuff."

Convinced that we had passed the "we're crooks and not cops test," Mario returned with the dope packaged for sale, and I handed him the green. As soon as he finished counting, Amos and I produced badges and Amos went into his "surprise-surprise" Flip Wilson routine.

Mario started laughing and jokingly remarked, "Those badges look pretty good can you get me one too?"

"How about we try this first Mario," as I produced hand-cuffs and began to hook him up. His face went mach 1 from frolic to fear.

In shocking disbelief he started yelling, "I asked you! I asked you!"

"We lied," Amos chimed in. "You been watching too much TV, bro. We don't have to tell you shit!" Mario went down for the count.

After we checked Mario into his deluxe accommodation at the gray bar hotel,

Amos and I drove to Norm's coffee shop at Beverly and La Cienega. I had spoken on the phone to a clean cut sounding chap named Andy, who was a friend of a friend of a friend who told him I came highly recommend and had plenty of money to keep my girlfriend happy. Andy sounded too eager and naive to be much of a dope dealer, and when we met face to face I was right. As we drove into Norm's, I told Amos to wait in the car, so we wouldn't spook Andy. I went inside and Andy was seated in a corner booth nervously nursing a cup of coffee. He looked to be about 30 to 35 with neatly trimmed hair, white shirt, and tie. He dressed for the occasion. I introduced myself, sat down, and made small talk.

"You in-pocket man?" as I gave him the cold emotionless stare, meant to put him off balance and convey the, "Don't fuck with me, fool" attitude.

Andy's Irish red cheeks got redder and his sweat glands started producing enough perspiration to fog a windshield.

"What do you mean, Frank?" his voice revealing a worrisome uncertainty.

"Do you have the stuff, Andy? Are you in-pocket or not?" I showed my impatience at his naivete. "How long you been dealing, Andy, since breakfast, or what?"

"You're my first score," he timidly responded.

Adopting a more brotherly tone, I asked, "Why are you doing this?"

Andy explained that his wife just had a baby, he was behind the eight ball in bills, and he hadn't sold a car in weeks at the Ford dealership where he worked.

"Maybe you ought to try Chevy's," I added with jovial wit. The sweat spigot turned off as I changed the tone of the conversation and he began to open up.

I felt like a priest in a confessional. I can't bust this guy, I thought, I couldn't live with myself.

"Okay, Andy babe, this is the big picture. Did somebody front you the two grams of blow or did you invest in the product yourself?"

"I bought it to turn a profit," he reluctantly answered.

"Do you believe in God, Andy?" I asked.

"Yeah, but I don't go to church much," he admitted.

"Sounds familiar," I thought to myself.

"Take a good look at my face. Have you seen me before Andy"?

"No," he answered, as his gaze met mine.

"Good, because today is the day the good Lord smiled upon you. Now you and I are going to go into the men's room, and you're going to flush the cash cow down the sewer pipe where that stuff belongs. You're going to leave here as fast as you can, and hope to God you never lay eyes on me again."

"I can't afford to loose what I invested. Are you a cop?" he asked in a confused hesitant tone.

"You can't afford not to, Andy. Do you think I'm fucking with you? I'm not fucking with you. Let's just say I'm you're guardian angel. Now let's get on with it."

I followed him into the can, and when the deed was done, he looked at me like a sinner looks at a priest after being granted absolution. He gave up an extremely heart-felt, "Thanks, man," and left. It may have been a hard-luck story, but I bought it. Now I would have to square this with Amos and the lieutenant as my recap numbers would now be one short. This was a compassionate freebie on my part. He wasn't evil, just desperate, and "there but for the grace of God there go I." In this case, a little mendacity with the bosses was good for the soul.

36 STEPS TO HEAVEN OR HELL (OR HOW I GET THERE FROM HERE)
The wayward wind is a restless wind
that yearns to wander · SUNG BY GOGI GRANT

t was 1958 and Pop (my father) had just turned the two-tone white-over-green Buick Special (the one with three holes distinguished from the more expensive Roadmaster with four holes) into the Calvary Cemetery from Queen's Boulevard. The stylish streamliner cruised on wide whites and everybody knew you had to check off the option box along with the deluxe hub cabs with Buick scripted in the center. The glistening chrome front bumper with its two over-stated bullet protrusions, called "dagmars" (after a famous stripper), was bold and muscular. The big Buick boasted the confidence of Dwight Eisenhower's postwar America which it reflected. Gogi Grant's voice was emanating from the Sonamatic radio beckoning the "Wayward Wind." You remember, a 1958 chart buster: "The wayward wind is a restless wind that yearns to wonder...." Pop turned the radio off, and Gogi's ramblings were temporarily silenced along with the thousands of souls whose gravestones marked the finality of their mortality. To this day I associate the "Wayward Wind" with New York's Calvary Cemetery. Pop said it was disrespectful to the dead to listen to music in the cemetery.

The Calvary is only a short distance from the 59th Street Bridge (which Simon and Garfunkle made famous in the song of the same name in the Sixties) and the East River, which divides the borough of Queens from Manhattan Island. Calvary is the largest and oldest cemetery of the archdiocese of New York. A sign greets all those who enter, "This Cemetery gives witness to the respect we give to the human body, even in death, because it is a temple of the Holy Spirit and will rise again to eternal life."

If one looks up from the graves of the dead in a heavenly direction, due north (well, maybe it's west, but anyway), the majestic Manhattan skyline comes into view. The whirlwind of the city's hectic bustle lies in sharp contrast to the solitary shady calm of the bucolic burial ground and quiescent repose of those buried there. They no longer have to deal with such trivial pursuits as news, weather, and traffic. Rushing about is now as irrelevant to them as Gogi's restless wind.

The real significance of the Calvary is that it's named for the Crucifixion. Sister Mary James told us in Catechism class it was at Calvary that Jesus suffered his sacrificial death on the cross by which He redeemed us for our sins. I wasn't sure what sacrifice meant, and I thought redeemed was about getting pennies back from the grocery store for pop bottles. All I really knew of Calvary was that it was where we went every couple of months to visit my grandfather and grandmother's (nono and nona's) grave.

It was the dead of winter, and we had to trudge through the heavy water-laden white stuff to reach their graves. The restless wayward wind was eddying through the trees.

This was the proper way of showing respect for the deceased. The grave stone was marked "Beloved Parents Salvatore DiPaola 1890-1923 and Celestina DiPaola 1896-1931. Even though I was only nine years old, I subtracted 1890 from 1923 and came up with grandpa's age when he died at 33. I then asked Pop how come nono died when he was only 33. Even to a kid who knew nothing about anything, it seemed pretty young anyway. Pop took hold of both of my shoulders in a fatherly embrace and looking deep into my eyes with a hint of sadness said, "I guess you're old enough to know the whole story. Here it is:"

When the steamship Regina D'Italia sailed from the dock at Palermo on October 2, 1910, the Island of Sicily soon disappeared into the horizon. One of those passengers watching the disappearing act was my grandfather, Salvatore DiPaola, age 24, marital status single, place of residence Borgetto, Sicily. That's what the ship's manifest matter-of-factly stated; a skeletal outline of brevity concealing a stirring range of human emotions. Hope and fear, promise and uncertainty, I'm sure were all part of the mix.

Borgetto was such a small village that it doesn't appear on most maps. Between 1880 and 1920 approximately fifteen million expectant souls left Italy for America, and it has been said that by 1920 more than one third of the population of southern Italy had immigrated to America. Much of this migration was due to the harsh conditions, extreme poverty, and lack of opportunity. The twelve-day sea voyage was no luxury cruise. Most of the immigrants were booked into steerage, the below deck section in the belly of the boat near the ship's steering mechanism.

"Thirteen days of hell" was how my Aunt Mary, who made the voyage with my grandmother, described steerage to me as a young boy. Each room was basically a storage closet that held four one-body bunks, two feet wide and six feet long. Steerage rooms were eleven feet by six feet, so do the math: not a lot of breathing room. And if you're claustrophobic, derangement or paranoia soon followed. Steerage passengers ('cell block inhabitants' is probably a better term) were not allowed to venture to the upper decks inhabited by the well-to-do first-class crowd. The cramped quarters smelled of human waste and were damp and dirty. Food often consisted of left over scraps from the well-heeled passenger's top side.

Crew members were often from Northern Italy and had nothing but contempt for the Sicilians and often did not understand their dialect. For amusement passengers in the upper decks would throw coins down below with an air of superfluous superiority and between ship-rocking waves watch their fellow travelers scramble for the coins like alley dogs fetching garbage snippets. Deception was also rampant as some of the craftier Sicilians, called sharpies" preyed upon the ignorance and naivety of their fellow travelers. They tried to swindle them out of their meager financial means with promises of connections to jobs or housing in America. The Regina D'Italia finally reached its destination, the port of New York, on October 15, 1910 and the thirty-six steps to heaven or hell would begin at the gates of Ellis Island.

The Statue of Liberty was ten years older than sweet sixteen when the young man from Sicily first gazed eyes on it on that October day. I can envision him making the sign of the cross and his brown eyes beaming with the joyful wonder that traveled down his face to form a huge smile that screamed, "Yes, I made it!" No, not quite; there was still the final exam, actually thirty-six final exams, before this journey would come to a successful end. If the immigrants passed all the thirty-six steps, bingo: the gates of heaven opened, and they were in.

A relative or friend had to vouch for them and assure the immigration officers that the new arrivals had employment and a place to call home. This insured they would not be a burden on their new country. An "F" on any one of the entrance exams would send them back where they came from. Heaven if they made it; hell if they didn't. Each immigrant also had to pay a two-bit head tax, which was included in the boat fee.

Ellis Island's three-and-a-half acres sit at the entrance of New York harbor a few dashing waves from the Statue of Liberty. Its French renaissance exterior of brick and limestone actually looks somewhat inviting from the outside, but pretty institutionalized from the inside. Five thousand people a day passed through Ellis Island, and all of them had to navigate the ominous sea of thirty-six steps. Between 1880 and 1920 approximately fifteen million people were processed through. The processing was more akin to sorting out cattle than welcoming newcomers to their nascent port-of-call and the rest of their lives. Many were turned back due to diseases such as farvus (a scalp disease) or at the eye inspection station due to the dreaded "trachoma," or red eye as it were referred to. To inspect for red eye, button hooks were used to roll over the eye lids. One can just imagine the look of horror on the already frightened faces as the resolute immigration officer approached them with the ominous hook in hand.

Each arriving immigrant, along with a confused look, had a ship's manifest tag pinned over their left breast, again a similarity to cattle. The inspectors had copies of each manifest and would match up customers accordingly. Batteries of test were given to measure the mental as well as medical competency to see if they were worthy of entrance. Quite a contrast to today.

Italians without the proper documents or whose names did not match up with the ships' manifests were labeled wops (without papers) and paraded to the "wop" holding area to be sorted out. Approximately 250,000 Italians were sent back to Italy between 1890 and 1920, after being poked, prodded, and often humiliated. Many of the immigration inspectors who did speak Italian were northerners, and their tongues were incomprehensible to the southerners with Sicilian dialects. Many of the Sicilians couldn't read or write, and not comprehending the king's Italian didn't help them win any bonus points. Immigrants who inspectors believed might be mentally incompetent had an "X" marked on their shoulder, indicating they needed further examination. The further examination could take two minutes or two hours – at the whim of the examiner. No, an immigrant's lot was not an easy one. Once the thirty-six steps were successfully hurdled, the adventure of a life time began, and the privilege of calling America their home came to fruition.

My nona, Celestina Chinese (pronounced Chenazee) was only fourteen years old when she arrived in the Promised Land on March 30, 1911. She hailed from the small village of Partinico, Sicily, near the port of Palermo. She was accompanied by her half-sister Mary Caruso, my great–aunt, who was only sixteen. Both my grandmother and Aunt Mary were adopted.

During the war, my father, after having seen combat in the invasion of North Africa and the Sicilian invasion as a proud member of the Second Armored "Hell on Wheels" Division, went on a recon mission to Partinico to sift out his roots. I guess you could call it "ancestery.jeep" instead of ancestery.com. When Pop rolled into the village square in his green machine and spit and polish khakis, everybody with the name of Caruso wanted to claim the G.I. with the Sicilian dialect framed with a New York accent as their own. Pop was an interpreter in General Patton's Third Army as well as a hotshot gunner with a fifty-caliber machine gun. Many of the town's folk were named Caruso but when he walked into one house and there was picture of his mother and Aunt Mary, he knew he had struck oil. Una tassa di caffe (a cup of coffee) and mangia, mangia! was the second order of business for the long lost relatives after numerous hugs and kisses. Pop was able to spend several days feasting on homemade spaghetti and vino, and then it was back to bullets and bayonets.

As the steamship Venezia was pulling into New York harbor, one can imagine the sun beginning to illuminate the Statue of Liberty standing guard over the intersection of two rivers sandwiching the island of Manhattan. The Lady was also welcoming the newcomers. The ship's belly was still dark and depressing, a sharp contrast to the sunlit Lady of welcome. Aunt Mary described the scene to me in her broken English and wide smile. The two teenage girls embraced each other in expectant jubilation as the cool breeze from the East River sailed over their smiling faces, a measure of brightness that must have filled their entire being.

The ship's voyage and the predators on board that the two teenage girls had to endure took its toll. Aunt Mary even at sixteen was no pushover and protected them both. As the girls disembarked, the Venizia became a miserable floating memory. The thirty-six Gestapo-like check points had the girls' emotions flip a u-turn from joy to fear. It was feared by the authorities that young women traveling alone would become prostitutes; therefore their sponsoring relatives had to vouch for them in person. My Uncle Diluvio was that person.

Little did Celestina Chinese know that in two short years she would be married to one Salvatore DiPaola, who had made the same voyage a year earlier. From what I could gather, the whirlwind romance between Celestina and Salvatore went something like this: Celestina and my aunt Mary were living with their Uncle Diluvio on the lower east side. Through some connections Uncle Diluvio got them a job rolling tobacco at a cigar factory on First Avenue. That's right; my nona was working at a cigar factory when she was fourteen. New York wasn't big on child labor laws at that time.

Everybody had to kick in because tenement living wasn't cheap, although conditions were squalid. My nona would exit the factory building daily at noon to eat lunch. This was about the same time that a fruit and vegetable peddler with an inviting smile and rugged good looks – my nono – would be navigating his horse and wagon through the streets teeming with bundles of humanity. Pushcarts and other peddlers who made up the New York street scene at the turn of the century joined the fray. Love must have been in the New York air, and, according to legend, the daily casual encounters eventually led to a brief courtship and marriage.

They began their life together in a two-room apartment in a tenement at 411 East 60th Street, a stone's throw from the East River. Tenement living was cramped and chaotic with privacy being virtually nonexistent. Often many families shared one bathroom and shower per floor, and it was not uncommon to bathe the baby in the kitchen sink. My grandparents would face new beginnings in a new land. They weren't rich in possessions or coin of the realm, but their love of each other and faith in God led to their profound optimism. That which lay ahead would be bravely faced together, the good and the not so good.

GUNFIGHT AT THE FIFTY-NINTH STREET STABLE

There is no greater love than to lay down one's life for one's friends.– JOHN 15:13

ost of the Italians were drawn to New York City, not only because of Ellis Island, but because it had become the biggest boomtown in modern history with a huge demand for cheap, unskilled labor. Many of them had worked the fields in the small towns that danced along the terrain of southern Italy and Sicily, or had fished the waters of the Mediterranean. There weren't many fields in New York City, so they had to adapt, and adapt they did.

Young Salvatore DiPaola could no longer grow fruits and vegetables, but with his knowledge of produce and a silver Sicilian tongue he could certainly sell that which he used to grow.

The young Sicilian came to New York with full blown determination, a strong work ethic, and a hearty, steadfast pride. Like many of his paisanos, he was a man of steel. You had to be just to survive, let alone prosper. I am forced to rely on the stories and hearsay of my great Aunt Mary and other assorted relatives, long since dead, of the old Brooklyn I knew as a kid growing up. More recently, the receding memories of aunts and uncles who still offer up talks pulled from faded childhood memories have helped paint the picture.

Nono's eyes were very brown, and based on too few old photographs, belied an endearing sincerity. My grandfather was a man you could trust and a guy you could like. The eyes told you so; they said it all. He was not a physically big man, but he was a powerhouse in the character category. He said what he meant and meant what he said. He was destined to forge through many obstacles until the final one. Young Salvatore was a vibrant guy, a man of generous heart and upright spirit who took life seriously, and even in his wedding photo he rarely smiled. (The same is said of me. Maybe it's in the genes.)

Most of the Italians settled in the area around Mulberry Street, which came to be known as Little Italy. The northern Italians were the first to arrive but were quickly over-whelmed by the Sicilians and southern Italians who were often poorer and less educated. The northerners felt superior. Prejudice was alive and well, so they escaped to other areas to what is now Greenwich Village, Chelsea, and across the river to

Jersey to remove themselves from the low-class guineas.

As the numbers increased so did the negative stereotyping. Salvatore was a man on a mission, too busy trying to earn a living to be bothered by guinea or wop prejudices. No self-pity here, just self-discipline. When times got tough, the tough got going. My grandfather would be up way before the rising sun, coupling horse to wagon so he could be at the terminal market at 1st Avenue and 70th Street early enough to get the pick of the produce. Competition ran thick among the peddlers who jammed the streets of the lower east side.

Their home at 411 East 60th Street was in the shadow of the 59th Street Bridge. At night, the lights which danced upon the span cast an ice-like sheen on the river and adjacent tenements below. Artificial lights from a bridge weren't the only things that glowed. Within the decaying paint-peeled walls inside the 1800's tenement, was a love that ran as strong and deep as the support pillars of the towering bridge. La familia was the central theme of this play book. As the love grew, so did the family DiPaola.

The time went by quickly, and within their first eight years of marriage they produced four children evenly spaced two years apart. My aunt Clara was the first of the new arrivals followed by my Uncle Vincenzo, my father Francesco, and baby Beatrice, affectionately called Aunt Bea. This was good. More years passed, the babies grew into children, and life went on. Three of them are still alive and lucid. Aunt Clara recently passed and joined her mother and father. The older they get the more cherished the memories of a by-gone era become.

Italian mamas understood their role well. It was a self-sacrificing endeavor of raising the family in a disciplined, virtue-based setting of maternal love and natural affection. Even at 16, my nona knew instinctively that she would ultimately be the glue which held the family together and kept it going. This is where the term mama mia is derived. She was the moral star of the family universe. Like a ship's rudder, she kept it sailing in the right direction.

In the spirit of most Italian woman of the day, the young bride and mother made her own bread and pasta. On special occasions, Pop remembers the home-made macaroni being placed on a large wooden cutting board scaniaduro, and each family member would scoop the food from the center to their piece of the wooden board and eat without plates. As kids they could always rely on their mama. Nona seemed to operate in a partnership with the Virgin Mary, which provided a sense of comfort and peace in the knowledge that everything would be okay. From an early age, the kids went to church and learned how to act and behave from the Virgin Mary and her Son.

My grandfather had the traditional role of bread winner. Shoe leather, horse's hoofs, and wagon wheels plodding along the cobble stone streets of old New York. Twelve hours a day, six days a week is how it went. The New York ghetto was a patchwork of narrow streets engulfed by over-crowded tenements packed thick with immigrant humanity who called it home. The flags of the tenements were a thousand clothes lines that blew white.

Living conditions were deplorable, but in spite of the obstacles or maybe even because of them, some Sicilian souls were able to break from the herd and actually prosper. Salvatore DiPaola was one of those souls. The hard work and sacrifice were slowly erupting into the American dream which he had envisioned. The young Sicilian eventually rented a store front where produce and groceries were sold. His days as a peddler were winding down. The mama and papa had bought a piece of land across the river in Brooklyn. There his paisanos would help him to build a house and raise the family in a proper way. Soon he and Celestina, along with their four bambinos, would no longer live in the most crowded place on earth and endure the misery of the ghetto. Other Sicilians believed in prosperity also, but their vision of success wasn't based on hard work, but on hard crime.

The New York ghetto produced men who were good and those who were not so good. Young Salvatore was the good. He extended credit to those down on their luck. If a family had a problem he was always there to help. In today's terms he was "good people." Back in the day he was referred to in Sicilian as u cristiano e un pessu di pane or a Christian who is solid like a loaf of bread.

Success for one person can also be an opportunity for another. That other was the notorious Black Hand, also known as La Mano Nera. Black Handers, as they had come to be known, were the extortion tentacle of the Mafia and mostly preyed upon other Italian immigrants. The imprint of the dreaded black hand would usually accompany extortion notes or kidnapping ransom requests left at victim's residences or place of business. The crowded New York ghetto provided enough victims to keep the thugs on overtime. Extortion, robbery, kidnapping, and murder were so commonplace in the Italian ghetto that the New York Police Department created the "Italian Squad." So much for political correctness.

One of those chosen victims for extortion was the man with the four kids who came to America and made good. He was a guy with a family and a business. He had something to lose. He would pay up or else. Salvatore believed that the paisanos had to take a stand and stop paying La Mano Nera. He was vocal about his beliefs; maybe too vocal. In Sicilian, low-life thugs were called schifoso. As a small boy, my father remembers his mother saying chisti su schifoso canusciut (these low-life's are mobsters). Whenever she spotted them, she would grab the children's hand and avoid them. The peddler with something to lose would pay up, the Black Handers figured. They figured wrong. Salvatore DiPaola was no chump and no victim. He bought a pistol, and when they came for him he would be ready. He would deal with them. That's what stand-up guys did.

The 2nd of December in the City of New York in 1923 was cold; cold that pierced the flesh and chilled the bones. It wasn't a good day for anything, not even for dying. For the peddler turned grocer, for the father of the four bella pichuida, for the husband of the angelic Celestina, it would be the 2nd of never.

The morning began like most mornings began in the two-room, third-floor tenement apartment on East 60th Street. Men with straight razors and a towel flung over their shoulder along with mamas and their pichuida shared serpentine lines. These lines were sometimes long, sometimes short, but always lines for their brief shot at the only miserable bathroom on each miserable floor. Even the simple task of a shave, shower, or bowel movement was an ordeal.

As the daylight of the dawn climbed into the apartment window, humanity stirred to life. It was a market day; the day to hitch up horse and wagon for the trip to the terminal. Extra meats and vegetables and the bacala fish would be needed for the family Sunday meal. Nono promised his seven-year-old Vincenzo, my uncle, that he would take him and the horse and wagon to market. The little boy had looked forward to spending the day with his papa.

Fate and destiny must have also entered the dim lit room that morning, maybe even joined by a sixth sense premonition. Nobody will even know for sure why at the last minute the papa let the ninio sleep. Instead of waking him to join the day, he kissed him ever so lightly on the top of his head, than bade his wife good-bye and left. Twelve hours later as the day's journey did a slow fade into darkness, Papa DiPaola, horse in tow, was about to enter the stable on east 59th Street in the shadow of the 59th Street Bridge. Caution grabbed him by the legs and man and beast came to an abrupt halt. It was then that he heard a commotion and peered into the manure-scented enclosure. His eyes cried terror.

It was a do or die moment. His friend James Giulio was being tied up and gagged after being robbed at gunpoint by three Black Handers. DiPaola was still in the stealth mode and could have left to summon help, but that's not what stand-up guys did. When those intense sincere brown eyes of his transmitted the image of his friend's peril to the brain, I'm certain that there was no actual thought process involved. He did the right thing; instinctively he did what he knew in the depths of his gut he had to do. He rolled the dice the only way he knew. The newspaper article in the photographs section gives the story, but not the whole story. He drew his pistol and fired at the schifoso. He engaged the bad guys in a deadly gunfight. The hero had met the villains in a smelly stable that his horse called home.

Papa's shots missed their mark. Horses and humanity panicked as more shots rang out. When the scifoso took aim it didn't turn out like in the movies. In reality, when the good confront the bad and the ugly, the good don't always win. The victors and the vanquished, sometimes the good become the vanquished and the bad get to live another day. Black Hander's bullets went where fate and destiny told them they had to go. My grandfather felt the hot breath of a death-baited bullet. The straw covered stable floor was no longer pale yellow at its entrance. It was now another pigment, the color crimson which is not supposed to be on stable floors oozed onto the landscape. A life saved and a life lost. James Giulio couldn't even help his friend due to the ties that bound him. Sometimes life begins in a stable, sometimes it ends there. This was another wop killing for the Italian squad. The case probably went cold immediately; we'll never know.

In those days, only the wealthy could afford the luxury of a funeral home, so the peddler, the papa, the husband, returned in death to 411 East 60th Street. For the other mamas, papas, pichuida, and his padrone (godfather) to visit and pay their last respects. Papa rested peacefully on the living room couch for two days. His earthly pilgrimage in the New York ghetto came to an end. Now another pilgrimage would begin, written in the wind of eternity. His body would rest in peace permanently at the Calvary. That's how they did it in those days.

Uncle Vincenzo and Aunt Clara will never forget the bullet holes in his face and chest. They had two days to let it paint a permanent picture on the canvas of death in their memory bank. Pop and Aunt Bea were too young to remember much of anything. Maybe it's better that way. The beautiful and angelic Celestina no longer felt beautiful or angelic. The endearing smile was gone, eclipsed by a sorrowful resignation and throughout her remaining years it never returned to the bella facia (beautiful face). Two days later the body of his earthly dwelling was put to rest. She still prayed the Rosary daily and images of the Virgin Mary and her Son still proudly adorned the melancholy paint-peeled walls of a once-happy home. Papa was in a better place. She always reminded the pichuida in a rote, prayer-like monologue. She didn't have to convince herself for her faith was golden. It was more for the children.

Celestina, the good wife of the good man, died five years later of pneumonia that came one winter along with the chilling frost. A profoundly broken heart that would never be put back together was probably more like it, but they had to put something on the death certificate. At age 16 my aunt Clara took over and raised the family to survive as mama had taught her. Tenement neighbors pitched in and helped out, but the City of New York had other ideas. They were about to intervene and cart the four DiPaolas off to the local orphanage. Aunt Mary came to the rescue and took the kids in, along with her own clan, until grandma Caruso came from Italy to take over. When Aunt Clara turned 18 and got married to my uncle Eddie he got more than the wife he bargained for, and that was okay. Grandma Caruso went back to the old country, and the DiPaola kids moved in with their older sister and her husband, Eddie, in Brooklyn. So that's the story of, "In the Beginning."

If there is a post-script, I guess it's this: We can never forget where we came from and the tough mamas and papas of God-fearing character and strength who sacrificed to do the right thing. They gave birth to the greatest generation. The little boy wept at the grave stone. He would make it right. He would become a cop.

SISTER MARY KNOCKOUT AND THE RELIGIOUS RIGHT HOOK
"Love the Lord Our God with all your heart and all your soul;
Love your neighbor as yourself." -MARK 12:28-34

St. Boniface Roman Catholic Church in Elmont, Long Island is on the border with Valley Stream where I grew up. The old church was a wood framed structure painted in a whiter shade of pale. It had a tall narrow steeple that pointed all the way to heaven. The early American house of God was reminiscent of the ones you see in picture post cards with the colorful New England foliage in the background. These colonial icons used to dot the towns and cities until stained glass concrete mega-structures became all the rage.

Elmont and Valley Stream sit on the border of the borough of Queens, which, the last time I checked, was still part of the City of New York. These two small towns were the official gateway to suburbia, where those who wanted to escape the city escaped to.

Pop, the third oldest of the DiPaola family, had returned from General Patton's army a handful of years earlier with a Purple Heart and a metal plate in his right arm that held together what was left of his ulnar nerve. After serving in the North African and Sicilian invasion, where he had to kill other Sicilians, and the bloody Omaha Beach invasion of D-Day, he caught a souvenir in the form of a German bullet. Body and bullet collided during a vicious hedgerow battle in the picturesque French countryside at Marqueray.

My father and my mother, Caroline Gugino, met while working for the Veterans Administration after the war ended. They were both from Brooklyn; he was from Canarsie and she was from Ocean Parkway. In December of 1948 they had me, a divine happening if there ever was one. Five years later they joined the gold rush to suburban Long Island. They weren't seeking gold, rather a two-bedroom, one-bath, ranch-style piece of the American dream.

Being a kid in the suburbia of the 1950's was a pretty good gig as far as I can remember. All the dads worked and all the moms stayed home to raise the kids. I never heard of the word divorce. A babysitter was only someone you saw on a Saturday night when your parents wanted to get away from you and go someplace fancy where kids weren't supposed to be. When adult company came, I was banished to my room. Since there was only one TV, and that was in the living room where the grown-ups were hanging out, doing grown-up type things, I entertained myself playing with my little toy cars. Cars were always a big part of my life, even then. Stay in your room, be quiet, and play with the cars. Children should be seen "briefly" and not heard; it was the official mantra of the day. When I acted up or got a little too full of myself, a good "lickin" followed, and then, you guessed it, back to my room and the little cars.

Once upon a time I was playing in the snow with my cousin Bruce. After we got tired of throwing snow balls at each other, I got the bright idea to throw them at grown-ups when they weren't looking. The great snow ball caper went something like this: Old Man Finnegan was a neighbor who lived down the block on Catherine Street. He was real old – in his sixties or something – and he would yell at us to be quiet when we were playing ball in the street. As Bruce and I were walking down the street, Old Man Finnegan's house came into view, and through the big bay window of his dining room, we observed him seated at the dinner table with his old battleaxe wife, who also yelled at kids. This target was too tempting to pass up, so Bruce and I went into attack mode. Under the stealth of darkness and dense shrubbery we closed in. Bruce chickened out at the last minute, so I became the lone ranger of the strategic snowball attack which was about to shake the evening calm. I only wanted to spook the goofy geezer not give him a heart attack. I threw it hard and fast with precision accuracy. Glass shattered; the old crow and his wife emitted horrific screams echoing the feelings of dreadful peril.

"I can't believe you broke the window!" Bruce yelled.

We both ran for our lives, but we left foot prints in the snow. The thrill and excitement were gone in 60 seconds. They were replaced by the intense fear of getting caught. Was this like breaking and entering? Even though the snowball entered and not me, I wasn't really well-versed on the elements of crime back then. Suppose the old crow got a heart attack and died of fright? I'd get life in the pen for murder. What if pop found out? I'd get the mother of all beatings; he'd definitely use the strap for this one. I felt like Raskolnikov, Dostoyevsky's character in "Crime and Punishment."

The high from the caper was replaced by extreme fear. But once that awful thing called a conscience kicked in, guilt joined fear, and the two got together to beat me up big time. On top of it all, I had to worry about going to hell, which is where Sister Mary James said you went for doing bad things. Nope, it wasn't worth it. The cops tracked me down and left it up to pop, and, you guessed it, the strap.

When I played it straight, life was simple in the suburbia of the 1950's. I walked to kindergarten at the Howell Road School, which was about a mile away, and sometimes rode my bike. Only a few of the moms drove, but even if they did, it didn't matter much because most folks only had one car and the dads used it to get to work. Only rich people, or those who thought they were, had two cars. Like I said, life was simple.

Back to St. Boniface and the road to Sister Mary "knock-out" in the first round. In the beginning there were actually several St. Boniface's, but the one that grabbed me the most lived in the fourth century and was quite a character. His story goes something like this: There lived in Rome a beautiful lady of well-to-do means, who had a way with men. Her name was Algae. I guess today she would be called a woman of easy virtue who made it big. Her powers of charm and seduction were usually a poison to those who fell under her spell of enticement, and their pockets were usually lighter as well.

Boniface was officially known as her chief steward, but a partner in crime and part-time lover was probably closer to the truth. Boniface would set up the suckers and Algae did the rest. Before hooking up with the lady of lust, Boniface was dutifully employed as a pick-pocket and con man. Not much redeeming quality in these two, just a certain honor among thieves. Boniface had a strong and strange addiction to wine, women, and whatever other form of debauchery that came along. Not exactly the stuff saints are made of. In the midst of her insidious, lewd, and licentious ways, Algae had a strange revelation. Maybe Divine Grace was playing its heavy miraculous hand. Algae's revelation involved a vision of hell, and her epiphany began. She was no longer on a road to perdition, but one of redemption.

She related to Boniface that they would have to alter the course of their lives from one of vice to one of virtue. At first Boniface thought she must have made a little too merry with the spirits of libation the night before and laughed it off. She pressed him that they would have to atone for their wayward ways. Eventually, Boniface too was blinded by the light and came around. A common belief in those days was that those who honor Christians who had suffered for Christ's sake would be redeemed of their sins and rewarded in heaven. The eyes of the Lord would be upon those who feared Him. They would also be delivered from death. Algae then sent Boniface on the morbid journey to buy the relics of martyrs and bring them back so that she and Boniface could properly bury them in a place of honor at her expense. It was the custom that martyr's bodies had to be purchased or ransomed from their executioners for large sums of money. Algae hoped this would be a quid pro quo, and that she and Boniface would go north, instead of south, when they died.

Before Boniface left on the morbid martyr journey of redemption, he humorously remarked to Algae, "What if my body should be brought back to you for that of a martyr?"

Algae yelled at him for making light of something so serious and sent him on his way. Boniface was a jester and viewed most of life's activities through the prism of humor, especially when he was relieving somebody of their money. Life was a game, and he was determined to play it, at least until now. He still had some doubts about Algae's new found faith, but I guess when the spirit calls you can't refuse. During the long journey from Rome eastward to where the church was being persecuted, Boniface refrained from eating meat and drinking wine. Not one who was accustomed to self-denial, this was a big sacrifice, but he figured it would help his soul to identify with the sacrifices of the martyrs and indeed with Christ Himself. Fasting was also a Christian custom of the time – cleansing one's self and atonement for sins.

When he reached Tarsus, Boniface dismissed his servants and went straight to the court of the ruthless governor, Simplicious, who was holding a tribunal for martyrs. The ancient Romans were not known for their civil rights agenda or humane treatment of prisoners. The tribunal was more of a torture chamber, with most of the defendants soon to become martyrs. One prisoner was hanging by his feet with his head over a fire. Another had his limbs stretched apart and yet another had his hands chopped off. Gruesome, sadistic stuff; you get the picture.

Martyrs were bold and courageous: for them it was an honor to die for one's God and what they believed in. When he viewed the horrific, macabre public spectacle of torture, Boniface the thief, con-man, scammer, and rascal underwent a miraculous metamorphosis in a divine soul-gripping moment. He became a soldier of Christ. As the torture was in progress, Boniface jumped in with both feet and fearlessly proclaimed, "Great is the God of Christians, great is the God of holy martyrs. O beseech you, the servants of Jesus Christ to pray for me that I may join you in fighting against the devil."

Now remember, Boniface was the kind of guy who wouldn't get out of bed if there weren't a buck or a broad in it for him somewhere down the line. It was an instant conversion inspired in heaven but made in hell. Governor Simplicious was outraged at this insult and asked Boniface who he was.

"I'm a Christian and nothing you can do can make me renounce the name of Jesus Christ."

The Governor was thoroughly insulted by Boniface's vitriolic tirade which pitchforked his soul. Simplicious, the not so good Roman governor, decided that Boniface needed a little pain and torture. This consisted of sharpened reeds being forced under his nails and boiling lead poured into his mouth. When Boniface refused to die, the governor from hell had him thrown into a pot of boiling oil.

Miraculously Boniface came out unscathed and un-boiled.

The mean and evil governor had enough of this Christian crackpot who wouldn't die so he ordered him beheaded. Before Boniface cheerfully presented his head to the big man with the big blade, he sorrowfully uttered a simple prayer for forgiveness for his sinful life and pardon for his executioner. He lost his head with profound dignity. His servants had to pay five hundred pieces of gold for his now two-piece body so they could transport him back to Algae. His premonition in jest to her now became a reality.

Although gravely saddened by the loss of her soulmate, Algae voraciously thanked God for Boniface's victory over evil and laid him to rest in a gravesite on the outskirts of Rome. The site is marked today by a marble tomb and adjacent chapel, a fitting repose and remembrance for such a dedicated and valiant soldier in the army of Christ. Algae led a penitent life, and dying fifteen years later, she was buried near Boniface. The tomb of Boniface was discovered in 1603. His feast day is May 14th. (That's one story of sinners and saints according to *Butler's Lives of the Saints, Volume Two.*)

Sister Mary James was the fiery commander of confirmation classes at St. Boniface. She was stern and uncompromising. In another life she could have been a drill instructor at Parris Island. (As I am writing this I was distastefully distracted by a TV news story on teenage sexting, and how oral sex is the latest rage among middle school kids. If they had had a nunzilla like I had, to provide a divine dose of appropriate bodily behavior, these kids' physical activity would have been confined to a gymnasium.)

Sister Mary James further admonished us that our conscience was the little voice inside our soul that told us the difference between right and wrong, and it would not let us forget when we went astray. "Jesus loves us, but He also has a good memory," she admonished.

The day that got me into big trouble was the day that Mary Ellen Rodgers, a cute little blonde with pretty pigtails, helped me tie the shoelaces on my new Buster Browns. That was the start of something new. She aroused feelings in me that I didn't know I had. I liked these new feelings. It was a sin to talk to your neighbor and a mortal one if your neighbor was of the opposite sex. Mary Ellen was of the opposite sex all right, from the pigtails to the cute little patent leather shoes.

The "no talking" warning had been loudly and sternly trumpeted only three minutes earlier, but boys will be boys. I never even saw it coming. It was like a shot in the dark. The clenched fist of the nun from hell (I'm being facetious) traveled like a piston on the power stroke. It made contact with its intended target, my jaw, with the velocity of an exploding bullet. My flapping jaw was no longer flapping. My silence was not golden but painful; the fist that transcended time and space made its point, literally. Crying came to mind, but only for a second. What would Mary Ellen think? What would the guys think? No, crying was definitely out. I would have to suck it up. Sister Mary James was now Sister Mary Knockout. Her habit made her look twelve feet tall. I was petrified. I had broken the eleventh commandment, "Thou shall not talk in class." I was on the "A" train to hell.

Sister scolded, "You will listen, and you will learn!" She then admonished the class, "If you're good you'll go to heaven, bad, it's the other place down there." Simple enough. "The sky is blue, don't argue what shade it is," were her parting words of wisdom.

My punishment was to write the two steps to heaven: "Love the Lord your God with all your heart and soul, and love your neighbor as yourself." She then added the golden rule, "Do unto others as you would have others do unto you." After a hundred times I think I got it. Conscience development came at a price; my ego, my pride, and lastly my jaw. No moral relativism here, just heavy-handed instructional criticism.

* * * * *

Back in the days of the fabulous Fifties there were tail fins and chrome, morality and discipline. Even in public school, Christian kids recited the Lord's Prayer while the Jewish kids maintained respectful silence. Nobody squawked. After all, it was all the same God. Discipline was the order of the day in public school as well.

Shooting your mouth off there may not have gotten you Sister Mary's closed fist, but a few swats from a ruler or a good shaking drove the point home. Not paying attention or forgetting a homework assignment was good for a stint in the corner with a dunce cap on your head. We were humiliated into doing right, and by God we did right. The smart kids got A's and B's, dummies got D's and F's. In math, I was usually in the latter grouping.

How you felt wasn't an issue, but how you performed was. Most of the men teachers were WWII vets, so you got the proper historical perspective. The emphasis on patriotism didn't run silent, but it did run deep. The U.S. was the greatest experiment which created the greatest country in the history of the planet. God had destined it to be that way and in God we trusted.

Back in those days, if it wasn't a stick-ball game, the frivolity consisted of hide and seek, bicycle riding, or cowboys and Indians. Whenever Mattel came out with a new six-shooter we were dueling with bad guys like Gary Cooper did in "High Noon."

Pop's generation, the greatest generation, sacrificed and left blood and bodies in every God-forsaken corner of this globe that had a name, as well as some places that didn't. They wanted to learn us well so we didn't screw it up. In case we forgot, the movie studios made sure that John Wayne and his Hollywood home boys filled millions of black-'n-white TV screens. Patriotism was everywhere, and the kids wanted in. Heroes were plentiful. Hell, I couldn't wait for my personally engraved Mickey Mantle baseball bat or the Yogi Berra official catcher's mitt. Walt Disney had the most effect on me; yeah, back then all of us kids wanted to don a coonskin cap and be Davy Crockett.

When we played cops and robbers, everybody wanted to be a cop. When we played cowboys, all the guys wanted to be the good guy with the white hat because the good guys always won. The Mickey Mouse Club and the Mouseketeers were all the rage on teeny bopper TV. Annette Funicello was the mother of all Mouseketeers, and all the boys fell in love with her. I was sure she would answer the letter that my mom helped me write, and when hers never came, I found what "heartbroken" meant. I still kept watching, though. It was an endless infatuation, and I was hooked.

When I was a kid, if you struck out during a ball game the coach yelled and then corrected you. Nobody gave you self-esteem; you had to earn it. Doo-wop and Dagmars died, Annette grew up, Detroit's tail fins, wide whites, and a child's innocence would take a slow fade into never, never land; the revolution – It's a coming! Somehow, somewhere in time it would all get turned around.

SIT-DOWN AT THE GOLDEN GUN
Why didn't you come to me first? – FROM *THE GODFATHER*

The Golden Gun on Queen's Boulevard was your basic low-life, sleazy Italian mob joint. You know the type: a bland brick building with a garish neon cocktail-glass sign on the blink. The front doors hung double, faced in aluminum with two round portholes. The tail ends of the not-so-inviting entry doors were sheathed in over-padded, cheap red vinyl. I always figured that was used to cushion the blow of the hapless chap who got bounced for stiffing a bar tab or cracking wise with the wrong guy. The booths were trimmed in imitation red leather that made funny, offensive noises when certain parts of the anatomy slid in or out. Ostentatious cheap mirrors hung large on the walls so that dames in tight skirts and teased hair could make frequent eye contact with themselves for up-to-the-minute mascara and lipstick fixes. They had names like Rose, Connie, and Marie, and were more often than not referred to as broads by the gumbas and lounge lizards that inhabited the place. These enticing Italian-teased hair jobs were the mandated arm candy for upcoming wise-guys and wannabes. The mirrors also helped the more paranoid patrons watch their backs.

A sit-down in mob vernacular is a not-so-friendly meeting to set an individual right for a perceived wrong or lack of respect; an attitude adjustment, Italian-style. Sit-downs are usually held in cozy little places like the "Gun" for purposes of intimidation and control. Trust me, it works.

I was just a clean-cut college kid working my way through St. John's University in nearby Jamaica, New York. I wasn't a grease ball. I didn't even wear pointy shoes. So what was I doing there, and why was I summoned to a sit-down with an aging capo? It all boiled down to respect – or more specifically – lack of respect. When I wasn't cutting classes at St. John's, or buried in a beer at Poor Richard's Pub across the street on Union Turnpike, I was actually one of those kids who worked his way through college.

The chosen vehicle for my hard labor was the valet parking business. I started parking cars in high school on weekends. To keep the coin coming in and to satisfy my gear head cravings, I was also a pump-jockey at the local Sinclair gas station three days a week when school let out. Dino, the green dinosaur, made Sinclair famous, and it made me a very greasy $1.25 an hour. Valet parking was on Friday and Saturday nights at the high-end Dover House Restaurant in Westbury. The Dover House became famous on Long Island when Burt Bacharach bought it in the 60's. One night he came in with his new bride Angie Dickinson and introduced me to her. She told me I was cute and gave me a peck on the cheek. She was perfectly coiffed and in a tight white dress that to a kid of nineteen left little to the imagination. Angie got up close and personal, and my teenage libido was never the same.

By the time I got into St. John's, I had acquired the Dover House parking concession for myself, along with a couple of other top-notch restaurants. My good buddy, Tony, helped me out big time and we became partners. He had the business savvy and charisma to make it work. Tony was like a teenage Donald Trump. He was my mentor from whom I learned the art of the deal and how to get happy in lucky-lady land. Tony was a walking tech manual for "Chick Scoring 101." He tutored me in the finer points of dating. Together we worked well. He was the big brother I never had.

There were over a half a dozen high school and college kids working for us. Pulling in three hundred bucks a week and driving a brand new 1970 Olds 442 convertible made me a big shot and a legend in my own mind. At twenty years old I was making more dough than my college professors who were teaching me how to make dough. I had the world figured pretty well and was on top of the game, at least that's what I thought.

The Hilltop Manor Restaurant and catering house on Long Island had a plum parking lot that handled over a hundred classy rides a night. The take in tips was the stuff dreams of bulging pockets are made of. I signed a contract with the house, put a crew together, and was ready to hit the lot running. The valet parking service I was to replace was run by a guy named Mack Manelli.

Being the stand-up guy that I am, I contacted Mr. Manelli by phone, introduced myself, and tersely let go in somewhat of an arrogant vernacular, "You're out, I'm in, and hope there's no hard feelings. Stop by and I'll buy you a drink sometime."

This was not exactly the way to win friends and influence people. A day later I got a call from a guy named Ralph who spoke in basic Brooklyn-ese.

The cordial conversation, as I recall went something like this: "I'm calling for Mr. Manelli. He wants to meet you. Be at the Golden Gun on Queens Boulevard Friday night at eight o'clock."

I remember responding that I wasn't sure if I could make it. The Brooklyn bruiser voice at the other end shot back with a quick, "That wouldn't be a good idea. We'll see you Friday night."

"How will I know who he is?" I asked.

"We'll know you." The phone went dead, and so did I.

Friday night came a lot sooner than it was supposed to. I wore a double- breasted jacket, stylish pleated pants, and a turtleneck. I wanted to look like I belonged in the "Rat Pack" and was not just a punk college kid. My confidence level was at an all time low, so I brought my buddy Vinny along for moral support. Tony would have been at my side on this one, but he was serving Sam, his Uncle, at basic training at Ft. Polk.

When we walked in, Ralph made us right away. He dispensed with any formal introductions. I was glad I brought Vinny along, since two bodies would be harder to dispose of. "You Frank?" he asked with that gritty gruff pitch.

Ralph, the mug from Brooklyn, was about two stories taller than me and as wide as a Cadillac. He looked like he had been thrown out of one ring too many, which left him permanently punchy and which seriously inhibited his happy genes. He made sure we noticed the ominous bulge in his jacket.

"Mr. Manelli's table is over here. Follow me. He's waitin' for you's." He said in his rich Brooklyn accent. His eyes gazed flatly from that not so amiable puss as he spoke. The booth was round in shape, like the disco balls which hung from the ceiling above. "Mr. Manelli, the kids are here," he announced with a chuckle. The intimidation was working, but on the outside I was determined to maintain a cool look of tough ambivalence. Just an old guy with a receding hairline and a potbelly, what's the big deal, I quietly reassured myself. The closer I got to the booth, the worse it got. Ralph ushered us into the booth and threw himself in on the end. We were sandwiched in with no escape route. Doo-wop Sixties sounds were playing in the background but the music wasn't what was occupying my frontal lobe at the moment. The fifty- plus capo had intense eyes and a menacing grin.

"Tu u capisci u Sicilian?" He asked me if I spoke Sicilian. I told him my grandparents spoke it in the house so I understood a little. We made some small talk and then it got heavy. "You're here because you failed to show respect. Who the fuck do you think you are calling somebody you don't even know and talking wise?"

Fear sat across from anger, and fear blinked. Vinny's arm was half way up to his chin, but the gin and tonic never made it and almost spilled over the rim as it came crashing down in panic mode. I had been nursing my Jack Daniel's, but now I needed all I could get, so I inhaled it like an old alchie. I didn't know what to say, so I kept my mouth shut. The disgruntled capo went into overdrive as the pock-marked palooka grinned wide.

"Do you know what kind of joint this is, Mr. DiPaola?" he calmly asked.

I squeaked out a nervous, "Yes, sir."

"Good, do you see how I'm treated here with respect?"

Again I squeaked out a nervous, "Yes." My glass now empty except for the ice cubes that kept rattling around as I played with the tumbler. Ralph squeezed in closer as if for the kill and put his arm around me.

"You real lucky, kid", tuna breath whispered affectionately in my ear.

Mr. Manelli ordered me another drink from Marie, the makeup queen waitress, and let go with the following admonition: "Now listen, college boy, and listen good, because you're gonna get a real education here tonight. Always know who you're dealing with in this life before you shoot your mouth off. Capisce?"

I told him I understood.

"The only reason you and your stupid friend are gonna leave here tonight is because you're an ignorant, wise ass kid. In other words, you're stupid. You caught a big break, but don't be stupid again, you capisce?"

"Yes, Mr. Manelli," I said in a voice soaked in humble resignation.

"Good. Now we understand each other; we together in the way we think. You know what last part of your name, Paola, means in Sicilian? The pay off, and you just got yours. You get to leave in one piece. How you like a job and work for me? I like you, you got balls, and you know how to make a buck. Ralph checked you out."

Tuna breath was now my best friend and knowledgeably added, "He got potential, Mr. Manelli, he got potential."

Mr. Manelli then added, "You tink about it kid. Take your time. Stick with us here, and maybe someday your name be "Don Cheech." (In Sicilian "Cheech" is slang for Frank.) I graciously thanked the capo di tutti and said I wanted to finish college, but would think about his offer. "You run your lots, and my company run mine. Anybody ever bother you, let me know. If you need a ride, Ralph here, he'll take you," Mr. Manelli offered.

"We're okay. Thank you again, Mr. Manelli. That's very nice of you, but we got wheels," I quickly replied. I listened, I learned, and I left with my life. For a New York second there I thought I was gonna be the second DiPaola to be killed by the mob. The wise guy with the receding hair line set me wise big time, and I was a lot more humble leaving then when I went in.

As Vinny and I hit the street, he said, "I thought you were gonna show him who's boss, you were gonna be the big man."

"Shut up, Vinny, shut-up," was all I could manage.

WOODSTOCK

I'm not trying to cause a big sensation...I'm just talking about my generation.
— PETE TOWNSHEND OF *THE WHO*

The term Mach One refers to the speed of sound; 1,125 feet per second, if you didn't know. But to a car guy with any amount of premium pump fuel in his veins, or grease in his gut, it means a factory souped-up Mustang with embossed graphics, dual exhausts, and a flat black hood boasting a menacing shaker hood scoop for bigger breathing. Nineteen-sixty-nine was a banner year for muscle cars and morons. Car guys tuned up, morons tuned in and turned on. Muscle cars were more about smiles per gallon than miles per gallon. Every red blooded American kid had to plunk down his hard earned coin for Detroit's latest and hottest barnstorming rubber peelers.

The only adrenaline rush needed was 0-to-60 in less than eight seconds and the smell of Sunoco 260. Morons got a chemical high framed in a purple haze.

Crazy Carl, my car crazy comrade of pedal stomping fame, had just become the proud owner of a 1969 red Mustang Mach One that August week-end in 1969. Crazy Carl went through Detroit iron faster than most guys go through a pair of Fruit of the Looms. His methodology was to either throw a rod during a spirited street race or end up on the losing end of a police pursuit. His black garrison belt matched the black oil slick which stood proudly on a narrow forehead that had lost a few bouts with acne.

Anyway, crazy Carl was proud of his moniker and lived up to it any way he could. Crazy Carl came up with the crazy idea of going to a hippie music festival in a place I had never heard of 100+ miles up the New York State Thruway in the town of Bethel, New York. His sole purpose was to "ring out" the Mach One, and see if he could collect a few more speeding tickets for his wall of fame. He also figured that he might get lucky and score with a hippie chick or two.

The only way I was going to sign on to this trip was if I got some wheel time and made nice with the four-on-the-floor. Halfway into the trip, I got to drive. Melt and burn was more like it; I took two deep breaths, kicked the gas pedal, and cranked it over. I slipped the stick in first, fed some throttle, and heads turned at the precious metal bathed in red. Fifty miles later we exited the thruway.

We joined thousands of other masses of metal in a serpentine line which snaked along two lanes of freshly paved blacktop through the lush green countryside of upstate New York. The bold and beautiful sleek red ride, with its cosmic black stripes, was conspicuously out of place. She was part of a pathetic caravan of has-been vehicles driven by long-haired freaky people with love beads and bongs. VW vans and long-discarded delivery trucks from a not so distant sanguine era were now debased with day-glow paint patterned in a psychedelic montage. Once-noble vehicles were relegated to rusting relics emblazoned with peace signs, flower-power logos, and hand-scrawled signs such as "New York State Division of Drugs and Sex."

Woodstock was to be a chemical event all right, filled with these "nowhere" men, making nowhere plans, with other nobodies. The Mustang screamed "bad to the bone." The hippie heaps boasted looser to the max. "God is dead" bumper stickers were thrown into the profoundly stupid mix of dysfunctional hippie regalia. I guess if God was dead, by deductive reasoning, so were His rules, morality, and commandments. "Anything goes" was the upshot. If it feels, good do it! Presumably that was the narcissistic message. The heavy rain, mud, and muck framed the weekend along with a heavy dose of demonic depravity. No house of the rising sun; more like the house of the bursting clouds.

The shiny Mach One was like a gladiator in full battle dress trapped in a holding pen with nowhere to go. We soon abandoned the pristine princess in a narrow clearing and made our way on foot to Max Yasgur's farm and the festival itself. With our short hair and straight-legged jeans that weren't shredded or torn, we were conspicuously out of place among the rag-tag bunch of fellow travelers. Obviously, shaving razors were in short supply and never made it into the back packs filled with the required amount of LSD, Mary Jane, shrooms, and assorted amounts of other little silly drugs needed for psychedelic euphoria. Patchouli oil was also a biggie for any hippie worth his headband. It was essential for the arousal of cosmic caresses with the opposite sex.

After a cumbersome locomotion, roving in the rain through hill and dale, we finally got to within an earshot of the profanity-laced antics on stage and its accompanying music. I actually enjoyed some of the music, such as Joe Cocker, Jefferson Airplane, and The Who. When darkness had delivered itself, we had enough of the psychedelic rhapsody in the rain. The sights, sounds, and smells of Woodstock were truly something not to behold or forget. As far as the eye could see, wall-to-wall humanity filled the landscape.

This was no field of dreams, however; it was more like a pagan pig farm. It was a fun fest all right for some, but it was also a tableau of depravity. People were getting place from drugs and booze, with volumes of vomit raining on remnants of what was once a verdant pasture. Those who weren't ...ng all over each other were preoccupied with passing out or hallucinating.

What was left of the festival had now become clothing optional. Naughty nudity was on ceremonial display. Hairy legs and arm pits, sex-crazed weirdos were fornicating like barnyard animals everywhere. It reminded me of a line from Dante's Inferno: "Look across the filthy slew: you may already see the one they summon, if the swamp vapors do not hide him from you."

I was really upset by what I saw – and smelled – at Woodstock. If this was sex and drug revolution, it did not auger well for the future of our species. Rebellion of the counter-culture was everywhere. The "in crowd" that I hung thick with could never figure what we all were supposed to be rebelling against. Most of the tripping transgressors were from good middle- to upper-middle-class families. And they preferred sex-'n-drugs in the mud to what they had at home? I didn't understand it.

Either by misadventure, stupidity, or hallucination, most of these rubes were escaping societal norms and destroying the best years of their lives. The Mach One was ready to rocket home, and so were its two straight-edged wheel men.

Twenty years later, in August of 1989, my then-local newspaper, The Pasadena Star News, featured me in an article entitled, "Woodstock Revisited, the 20th Anniversary." Marci (I don't remember her last name) the reporter who came to my home for an interview, was a pretty, young and over-eager 20-something. Submerged under a set of bubbly baby blues was a smile full of optimism.

"What was it like to be a part of such a giant happening, and how did it change your life?" she asked hopefully.

I immediately turned off because she was so turned on. I didn't want to insult or dissuade the joyful journalist, but it was important that she get the real story behind what she came thinking the story was. The truth be told, Woodstock was a cesspool of immorality which to healthy eyes was dehumanizing and disgusting.

My response was far more sardonic than what she expected. Like half the planet, she drank too much of the happiness kool-aid and bought the hippie hype. The slick and groovy free spirit side of the late 60's tasted honey sweet to a lot of folks, but the backstory, and its inevitable results, ultimately smacked sour.

I began the monologue by asserting that if I were describing Woodstock in Biblical terms it would go something like this: "The weekend of August 15,1969 on a farm owned by a guy named Max Yasgur was a grandiose festival of fools. They laid waste to the land, poisoned their minds, and degraded their bodies. False idols inhabited their souls. They worshipped themselves; acid-head rock stars were their gods and prophets. The crowd was filled with lost, wasted wayfarers who were hungry and longing for...for what they did not know."

I told her that in my view Woodstock was basically a political protest littered with drug-induced delights in a lewd orgy of carnal consumption framed in acid-laced rock. Tattered American flags were used as blankets and muddied in a disgusting display of disrespect. Viet Cong flags flew on make-shift flag poles. I found this pathetic exposition of anti-Americanism was really disturbing. The evening newscasts at the time were filled with graphic reports of the carnage our soldiers were enduring in Vietnam, and these nihilistic Neanderthals were wrapped in a vibe of lyrical anti-establishment sociopathy.

I was trying to impress on the roving reporter that these counter-culture ghosts of the not so groovy side of the 60's were slowly infiltrating the establishment, and indeed were becoming the establishment. The knuckleheads I saw and smelled at Woodstock had morphed into mid-life yuppies and slithered into the power structure they had once so detested. The whole sex-'n-drug free spirit fiasco was a new reality-morality melt down of rag tag rubes chasing, or being chased, by Grace Slick's "White Rabbit."

Woodstock and the whole hippie free-love farce – if it feels good do it – was a great escape from everything remotely resembling sanity, restraint, or responsibility. Do the right thing was replaced by do your own thing. The not-so-groovy psychedelic generation got it all wrong. The greatest generation which preceded them got it mostly right. Had it not been for their struggles and sacrifices the heathens wouldn't have had the freedom to do it in the road. (Of course, the greatest generation parented the Woodstock generation, but for the life of me I don't know how or why.)

That's just what our enemies in the real world hoped for. If it weren't for their parent's generation, they would be goose-stepping to "Mein Kampf." Tokyo Rose would have stolen the show from Janis Joplin as the lead female vocalist. And she wouldn't be singing with Big Brother and The Holding Company, just with "Big Brother." I know she probably had enough of my rambling diatribe, but the cylinders were just getting cranked up.

I told young Marci that I didn't remember much from my college days at Long Island's Hofstra University (which I talked my way into after flunking out of St. Johns, my mouth roared and the dean bit), but one particular political science professor left an indelible mark on a layer of gray matter submerged under a rather dense cranium. It was a lecture on communism and the communist party in the United States. By the early 1960's the communist party was in the doldrums with undercover FBI agents outnumbering actual members at most meetings.

To increase the number of recruits to the commie cause, Gus Hall, the party's flamboyant leader, decided to focus not only on infiltrating labor unions, but the emerging peace movement as well. Under the guise of peace and social justice issues, college campuses were the perfect target of opportunity. I have no doubt that there were more pinkos than patriots in attendance that August weekend.

The reporter continued to listen in respectful silence. I told her that if someone is perpetually stoned and preoccupied by gratifying fleshy nerve endings, logic becomes elusive. Hippiedom's mantra of "tune in, turn on and if it feels good do it" could have been coined by Gus Hall himself. Actually it was Timothy Leary. More bongs, fewer brains make the sheep grow fonder. Anyway, I definitely gave her food for thought and ended the interview in true Walter Cronkite fashion, "And that's the way it was the weekend of August 15, 1969."

Marci's cheeks beamed bemused and quizzical. My take on Woodstock wasn't what she expected when she rolled in. She was very polite and gave me a fair shake in the article, even making mention of the excess of sex and drugs and their societal effects twenty years later. Colleges in the Sixties were already starting to spread the seeds of secularism. One sociology professor professed in class that the Ten Commandments did not apply to us today but were given to the ancient Israelites as rules of behavior for them.

I like to think of myself as a pragmatic optimist, but the profanity-laced echoes of Woodstock still ring perversely loud in some corners of our nation. In the true Woodstock spirit, as of this writing, a San Francisco city supervisor proudly blurts out profane rhetoric, especially the "F" word at supervisory meetings. At a recent San Francisco protest to ban the introduction of a nudity law, protestors shouted, "Keep San Francisco Nude and Lewd." A high school proudly proclaimed the good news that gun and drug use are down. In Colorado, a law making pot legal was passed: welcome to the legally-stoned generation. A prominent politician recently suggested that a statue be placed at Woodstock to celebrate the event. Really?

Drug use is so problematic and pervasive in today's society that the so-called "war against it" is virtually a lost cause. It's costing trillions in dollars and human lives, and it undermines the very fabric of our society. Sexual promiscuity is so common place that a dinner time TV commercial is more sexually explicit than a 1950's porno flick. Almost no lunatic behavior is off the table today. For those of you under forty, guess what? It wasn't always that way. The way it is today ain't the way it ought to be. No, there were no pot shops coming to neighborhoods near you. Yeah, there's always been immorality and wicked behavior, but it didn't masquerade itself as an indelible right or the new normal. In other words it wasn't okay.

I echoed all these profound sentiments and more as a guest narrator in a documentary on LSD guru, Timothy Leary; a 1995 film entitled, "Timothy Leary's Dead." His advocacy of the mind altering LSD ("little silly drug") at Harvard in the 60's showcased the drug world to thousands of young minds made of mush. It became cool to "tune in, turn on, and tune out" to quote the man himself. I appeared in uniform in the documentary where I spoke about Woodstock and its lasting effects on the social and moral order, and my observations both as a cop and a member of the human race. Looking for the white knight or the "White Rabbit?" You don't have to look too far. In a line I'll steal from a 60's group called the Buckingham's, who weren't at Woodstock, "It was kind of a drag."

Woodstock was a power primer for perversion. The most disturbing thing about the whole thing was that of the 500,000 souls present, profanely insane behavior was the norm, and sane normative behavior was at a minimum. The paradigm did a 180. Crazy Carl and I, who were somewhat normal, were not the norm there; we were the outcasts.

Today forty years later, we can see the ramifications of the Woodstock mentality everywhere. Born in the 1980's several cable TV stations brought gangster rap, with its violence and female degradation, along with lusty licentious rock videos into our homes. This was the start of an explosion of decadence which we see today. A disgusting parade of noise with titles advocating cop-killing and degrading the police tore up the tracks of sanity and decency.

This perverse poison and the low life "artists" (I use the term loosely) have become billionaire moguls, role models, and social icons by the mayhem media. They are even courted by prominent members of the community and politicians alike. Whether due to ignorance, or because they, like the kids, have drunk the kool-aid of cool. Several of these albums, in a total affront to rock and roll, have made the rock and roll hall of fame. Rock and roll originally consisted of melodies with lyrics of love that elevated women. Adjectives such as "cherish, worship, and adore" have been replaced by "bitches" and "whores." Back in the day, "Kissing and hugging in the back seat with Fred" were about as risky as things got.

In a recent court case, a seventeen-year-old stripper was allowed to continue stripping in a night club, and the club was not cited because the judge ruled that citing the juvenile would violate her freedom of expression. This kind of thinking, especially by a judge, is completely devoid of morality and common sense, sucked out like coke through a straw from the hippie playbook. In a saner time the club would have been closed and the juvenile taken into protective custody.

A recent story on school curriculums taught middle school kids about cross-dressing and that it was perfectly fine to express themselves. Condoms and cucumbers anyone? Marriage before childbirth? Maybe. How old-fashioned! The counter-culture is alive and fundamentally dangerous; on a mission to strip America of its God, virtues, and Judeo-Christian heritage. As the character mister Fezziwig expressed in the Dickens's "A Christmas Carol:" It's to preserve a way of life that one knew and loved."

Not too many months after Woodstock, I enlisted in the United States Army Reserves, and found myself enjoying a sweat-soaked six months of discipline and a daily diatribe of "You ain't back on the block, boy," at Ft. Dix in New Jersey. Due to the Woodstock-inspired anti-military sentiment of the day, we avoided wearing our uniforms in public. I served my country proudly for seven years and was honorably discharged at the rank of sergeant.

It took Rome five hundred years to self-destruct. Woodstock was a signpost to where we are today. The times they are a-changin'!

POLICE ACADEMY 1, 2, AND 3

You are never a loser until you quit trying.
— WILL ROGERS

The Los Angeles Police Department's reputation was built mainly by two men; one was a cop, and the other was an actor. The legendary Chief William Parker took a corruption plagued, undisciplined police force of the 1930's and 40's, and brought it into the 1950's with a complete make over. Military-type training with an emphasis on high entrance standards and discipline turned it into the world's finest big city police department. Internal Affairs was added to weed out corruption.

The infamous "Hat Squad" was created to rid Los Angeles of organized crime. Hat Squad detectives would meet big bad gangsters from points east at the airport, tell them they weren't welcome in big L.A., and re-route them on the next flight home. Big Bill Parker's philosophy was, "If they were gangsters they had no rights." The emphasis on tough professionalism did indeed turn the LAPD into a model for all law enforcement to follow, and it drew prospective recruits from all over the country.

I was one of those recruits. Jack Webb, the second most important person in the making of the image of the LAPD, convinced me. Through his TV hits of "Dragnet" and "Adam 12," the image of the LAPD became legendary and gave the department top billing on the national scene. LAPD was like the Green Berets of law enforcement. I grew up on a steady diet of these cop shows and newspaper articles that – even in New York – touted the LAPD's pro-active crime fighting techniques.

LAPD was now my chosen career path. In 1974, I left New York on a jet plane and several months later attended the very police academy that had been featured countless times on television. They told us during orientation that only one out of every one thousand applicants who applied actually made it through the entire process to become a full fledged Los Angeles police officer. Long and tough odds, but I was a betting man.

* * * * *

"Choke him out, Zorba, choke him out. Make the little wop's eyes bulge. He's not out yet, keep up the pressure. You're faking DiPaola, you're faking. Keep the pressure on, Zorba! Don't ease up, or I'll ring your neck," barked officer McMuscle, our P.T. instructor.

P.T. officially stood for physical training, but "pain and torture" was more like it. This training was about pushing through the pain and gaining intestinal fortitude. Academy training consisted of combat wrestling and horrendous physical work outs. The manicured green grass of the P.T. field was beaten down hard by too many LAPD recruits fighting for their dignity and their job. Sergeant McMuscle was a mountain of a man, and his breath shouted the crippling fear of merciless authority. Sergeant McMuscle had a physique with strong features that were well defined. His years of work outs with heavy metal definitely had produced the intended results.

As recruit officer Demetri Dephanopolus's fabulous forearm and bulging bicep closed in on my hapless neck he whispered, "I'm gonna lock it up so make it look good." I didn't see stars but my Adam's apple was never the same.

"Change partners," McMuscle barked.

It was now my turn to subdue Demetri Dephanopolus, in our game of officer and suspect. Demetri was of proud Greek heritage and resembled Anthony Quinn's character "Zorba the Greek." Hence, the P.T. staff took to calling him Zorba.

"Suspect get away," roared the lion of the lawn. Zorba wasn't quick due to his solidly squat frame, but he was strong; thus the nickname "bulldog Zorba." Once I got him in the bar-arm control choke hold, he was like a no-neck monster; a bucking bronco rider at the local rodeo. I went along for the bump and grind. Zorba was a true gentleman, and instead of pummeling me and making me one with the crab grass, he went easy.

I got my chance to return the favor and do Demetri a solid (favor). It was on the sweat-soaked five-mile runs through the smog choked hills of Elysian Park. As Demetri used to say in his self-deprecating manner, "Fat boys can't run." Endurance finally succumbed to fatigue on the infamous and appropriately name "cardiac hill." Demetri's shoulders started sloping, and his run started falling to a lethargic jog as his legs grew heavy. His arms were no longer strutting proudly, but swung loosely. The red and white Los Angeles City rescue ambulance waited down below for the casualties of "cardiac hill." Sergeant McMuscle barked unmercifully, "Nobody quits or walks, even if you pass out, the two closest recruits will be your support. Everybody finishes the run."

I pulled up alongside Zorba, and his eyes were starting the journey of the backwards role, where body and bone would soon connect unpleasantly with the ground below. I grabbed the big Greek and told him to hang on. "I've got you, brother. You're gonna make it." Another recruit grabbed Demetri's other side, and like a ruptured duck, he came home to roost. He finished the run.

Over the next two months Zorba the Greek and I formed a mutual admiration society. "Water seeks its own level," he would often say as we toasted our newfound camaraderie. The bond would never be broken, but it would be tested. Demetri was always there for me, and me for him. Demetri Dephanopolus was the kind of guy who would give you the shirt off his back. He was a right guy who embodied the LAPD motto of pride, integrity, and guts. I was honored to be his friend.

Demetri was particularly helpful to me with the remedial baton training so I could get all the sequential moves right. It wasn't a billy club or a night stick, Sergeant McMuscle would always remind us: it was a baton made of second growth hickory. We weren't to use it in a "nine from the sky" – actually beating someone in clubbing fashion – as east coast departments did. We were the Los Angeles Police Department, proud and professional. We were to use the baton in short, well aimed strokes, emulating the symmetry and poise of a ballet dancer.

"Through these doors pass the finest police officers in the world." This sign still hangs proudly above the entrance to the main building of the police academy, across from Dodger Stadium, in the verdant hills of Elysian Park. We weren't "pigs," as demonstrators would call us – among other names – but P.I.G's, which according to McMuscle, boastfully, stood for Pride, Integrity, and Guts.

Back to "cardiac hill." McMuscle said Los Angeles police officers aren't born, they're made, and it was up to him and his fellow Neanderthals to make them strong. "The more you sweat here the less you'll bleed on the street," he drummed into us daily. "If you quit here, you'll quit in the street, so quitting during P.T. was never an option."

∗ ∗ ∗ ∗ ∗

Zorba and I started hanging tight with another recruit named Adolph Anjou. What made Adolf stand out was not only that he was black, but that he hailed from Haiti and spoke French. Adolph and I were kind of like weeds on a manicured golf course. At the time the height requirement was 5'8" with no room to spare, and Adolph made it with a whole half an inch left over. When you threw in our accents, Adolph and I just didn't seem to fit in with the rest of the herd who sported the Midwestern or California laid-back lingo.

On the weekends, we worked out, had a few pops together, and perfected our spit shines. Since Demetri had been in the Marines and done time for his great Uncle Sam in Nam, he was our military maven. Demetri was the only one of we "big three" who was married, and he and his wife Kathy made generous in the domestic dining department at their home in Santa Monica. As the weeks dragged by, recruits were dropping out faster than mosquitoes from a barbeque bug light. For some of them it was the academics or strict discipline but mostly it was the physical training. Several recruits had been terminated because they got into off duty capers trying to play cops, or flashing their identification cards to get out of a jam. We didn't have badges or guns, because we weren't real cops yet.

Even though I thought I was in respectable shape, it wasn't respectable enough, and I was afraid the bell would soon toll for me. My morale did the "deep six" during one tumultuous torture session which combined running, combat wrestling, and whatever additional sadistic activity the P.T. staff could come up with. "Why don't you go back to New York and join the Mafia or something, DiPolio, or whatever you name is," yelled McMuscle in derisive mockery of my ancestry. The humor was lost on me.

After the Friday fallout I felt like getting fried, so I hit a club called Tiffany's in Marina Del Rey near my apartment. The bartenders there had become very dependent on Adolf and me, but since Adolf had other plans that night I sailed solo. Adolph's other plans consisted of a tall, leggy red head attached to the most flirtatious face in the whole Marina. Adolf loved cars, especially the fast and furious Ferraris, so he called her his testa rosa. Adolf loved white women more than he loved life itself and always had at least two or three on the arm. Even though Tiffany's was crowded, I was in a lonely place. My longevity in Elysian Park wasn't looking too good, and I knew it.

The band was loud ,but not loud enough to drown out two loud pops that sounded like gun shots. The sound traveled from the doorway to the bar where I was sourly nursing my second Manhattan. I straightened myself up a little languidly and threw a glance to where the loud pops had traveled from. Being all too familiar with the sound of gunfire from the daily shooting range routine, I thought I was hearing things. Between me and the Manhattan, I thought I was imagining it. I wasn't. A tall fellow with broad shoulders and wavy black hair was standing over another guy who had been felled by the pops that interrupted my liquid indulgence mid-sip. The bouncer had a death grip on the shooter's hand trying to wrestle the gun from him. I flew off the stool and sliced threw a group of luscious lollipops who were showing more "T" and "A" than should have been legal. I leapt into action Superman style. I was small but quick and climbed onto his back so swiftly he never knew what hit him. My arms formed a vice grip on the neck though there was very little of it between his chest and his head. As his carotid artery compressed, the lack of blood feeding his brain made his lights go dimmer. The chokehold I had practiced a hundred times was slowly having its intended effect, except for one slight problem. The revolver in his hand was trying to reach around and shoot me.

"Get the gun! Get the gun!" I shouted frantically at the bouncer. The shooter was big and powerful, outweighing me by a good forty pounds. Choking him out, as his neck and I hugged, seemed like a slow-motion movie clip. The big lug finally tumbled like the New Year's Eve ball. His knees danced as he surrendered to the hard wood floor. The bouncer grabbed the gun, and the brain fade transported him in to the big sleep. There was confusion and yelling, but one thing was for sure, I had to get out of there before the cops came.

Lieutenant Adam's voice resonated sharply in my head: "Don't get involved in anything off duty, or it could lead to your termination." So I bolted with the barflies and was gone in a flash. I learned later that the big man was a mobster from back east, and the victim was a targeted hit. The victim lived. I did good, real good, but it was a stupid thing to do. I could have been killed. You don't take a choke hold to a gun fight.

We were coming up on the eighth week and the dreaded "black Friday," the do-or-die of recruit officer training. If they were going to wash you out, this was the day of reckoning. After a brutal P.T. test workout, I failed to control and cuff my recruit officer suspect, as required.

"You don't have what it takes to be a Los Angeles police officer. Get your hat and books and go see the lieutenant," said one of the P.T. staff. The dreaded words stung like a thousand bees. I was dejected and rejected. I had let myself down big time. What do I do now, go back to New York or stay in big L.A.? I never blamed the academy staff, just myself. They had standards that had to be met.

These were the days just before affirmative action, but it wouldn't have mattered much. White males of Italian heritage weren't part of the discriminated "let's lower the standards" crowd. Unfortunately, a few years later rules were bent, standards lowered, and quotas implemented. The country changed, and so did the LAPD. An L.A. city councilman recently remarked, "That it's not your father's LAPD anymore." Too bad, I thought.

Adolph and Demetri tried to help me through the weekend with the assistance of some very competent bar tenders, but it didn't work. I now suffered from the "3 D's:" drunk, dejected, and depressed. When I got over my hangover I saw a billboard which read, "Make a difference and join the LAPD Reserve Corps." Reserve officers had to attend a nine-month academy on weekends and two nights a week in order to graduate. It was designed for people who had full time jobs and still wanted to be part-time cops. They had to work a minimum of two shifts monthly and received fourteen dollars (gas money) a month as a recompense for their effort. LAPD gave me credit for time served, and a week later I was back at 1880 N. Academy Drive in Elysian Park. When the same P.T. staff saw me in formation they did a double-take.

"You got a lot of guts kid. You must be a glutton for punishment," McMuscle sneered.

Five months later I graduated and was assigned to Newton Division, or "Shootin' Newton," as they called it, and for obvious reasons. Newton covered from downtown Los Angeles' Seventh Street south to Florence in the heart of South Central, better known as Watts. Newton was a division that tested you and was exactly what I needed. I got a day job as a head hunter just to pay the rent and played cops and robbers nights and weekends, working about ten shifts a month. Most of the cops thought I was a regular since I was around so much. I needed the confidence to know I had the guts and intestinal fortitude to be a Los Angeles police officer. Working the streets in one of the toughest divisions in L.A. gave me that. Newton became famous for the S.L.A. shoot out in 1974 at 54th and Compton.

I was to learn firsthand how "Shootin' Newton" got its name. My partner and I responded to a radio call of a "disturbed man with a gun." I was disturbed, too, when a bullet and my brain almost collided. I ducked and weaved in a dance with death and finally took the suspect into custody. I had what it took to survive.

LAPD in the Seventies policed the city of three million with only seven thousand cops. This was the lowest ratio in the country, and L.A. had one of the lowest crime rates. We were extremely effective because of a high degree of professionalism and being proactive instead of just reactive. Los Angeles police officers were trained to look for criminals and intervene before crimes happened. It was different back then: cops drank their coffee hot and black at Winchell's on the idling hood of a battle-scarred black-'n-white. No sipping vente, grande, mocha, jumbo-java lattes at Starbuck's. Most cops smoked cigars or cigarettes, and the country boys chewed tobacco.

We took care of business on the street in a no-nonsense manner, and respect and fear were the buzz words for the bad guys. No political correctness in this department, not then anyway.

Almost a year to the day after the big academy wash-out I returned to the Los Angeles Police Academy for the third time to become a full fledged police officer. I had worked out all year and was in great physical shape. Once again, the P.T. staff was floored, "You're definitely no quitter, are you kid!" McMuscle and the boys good-naturedly offered up. It was my destiny to become a Los Angeles police officer, and become one I did. Even though I had the dubious distinction of having the most academy time in history, I finally made it. My graduation on that same field where I had left so much sweat and blood was the proudest moment of my life. Chief of Police Ed Davis (Crazy Ed) pinned the oval icon of courage and might which Jack Webb made famous, on my chest. My date with destiny had arrived. Prayers answered, a dream realized, and a purpose-driven adventure about to begin. I would be protecting and serving in the City of Angels.

FROM MEXICO WITH LOVE — A TALE OF TWO PEOPLE
A successful marriage is always a triangle — a man, a woman and God.
— CECIL MYERS

My friend Bobby-boy and I were out for an evening cruise in my new Porsche 911S. The bronze metallic paint complemented the perfection of its magnificent fit and finish.

Borla exhaust provided just enough purr for the understated sex appeal of the four-wheel roller coaster. I tooled the 911S onto San Vicente Blvd. from Wilshire, which turned out to be a propitious move. A Kelly green flashing neon shamrock indicated Tom Bergan's Irish Pub was just up ahead. Bobby-boy suggested that a bit of Bushmill's and Blarney might be just the right touch to begin the Friday night festivities. Tom Bergan's had a reputation for serving the finest Irish coffees in town. The whipped cream that topped off the hot and black soul warmer was carefully blended by Irish artisan hands. It had just the right consistency so the cream didn't sink, but floated on top providing the appropriate ivory touch to the ebony below. After all, it had to entice the eye as well as the palate, stirring the senses like the scent of a beautiful woman. The pub fare and libations were top drawer, and so were the patrons of the opposite sex.

My eyes were on red alert for the pinnacle of parking spaces perfectly suited for the (mechanical) lady from Stuttgart, when they feasted on another lady. Actually two; a blonde and a brunette; the pair were hurriedly making their way down the last patch of sidewalk which led up to the doorway. I had to think fast or lose them to the crowd inside. I swung the Porsche up a driveway and hit the brakes just as they approached. The car now formed a barrier blocking their path. The blonde started walking around the nose with its sloping front end, but the brunette was bolder.

She turned her sweet face toward me, and as contact was made she annoyingly asked, "Will you please move so that we can pass?"

She had large, endearing brown eyes that knew how to pierce a heart and probably anything else she wanted to penetrate. The eyes belied a sincerity and dignity that was genuine, yet intriguing with an added hint of mystery. The brunette was framed beautifully, emphasized by a dark blue velvet blazer and bright red blouse that complemented her lipstick of the same color. Her hair was an enticing shade of amber and a touch of red was added to a set of pallid cheeks. I wanted to get to know this beautiful lady but it wasn't for all the usual anatomical reasons. She was sexy in a discreet, understated way – stunning, yet angelic.

"Can you please move the car so we can pass?" she said again annoyingly with an edge to her voice and sarcastic smile on her lips.

I was far from being my usual glib self and came up with some dopey line like, "There are two of you and two of us, why hassle with the crowds inside? It doesn't get any better than this, and we can go to the Holiday Inn on Sepulveda, you know the one with the revolving bar on top where it's quiet and we can get to know each other."

"Maybe I like the hassle, and no, I don't want to go to any Holiday Inn," she made a quick comeback. This brief encounter on a moon-lit Westwood Street was not going my way.

The blonde had already circumnavigated the car and showed her obvious disinterest in us with an irritating, "Forget them, let's go."

I asked the beautiful brunette for her name and phone number after introducing Bobby and myself.

"I don't think so. I have to go," she responded.

As she started to walk away I let the clutch out, just a little, and the Porsche crept forward enough to again block her path. "You're beautiful and I would like to see you again," I added desperately. She stopped walking and stopped smiling, she was almost tolerant. So I added, almost pleading, "Listen, I don't blame you for not wanting to give me your number but I'm a cop with LAPD, not Jack the Ripper, so how about it?"

The woman who defined what it meant to be a lady finally succumbed. "Okay, I'll give you my work number, and then I have to go."

I hastily wrote down her name and number and she was gone. She was like polished silver, and sense number six told me that this lady was different. She would tell me later that she asked her blonde friend, "What did that guy look like?" and her friend responded, "Just another short haired turkey." In my haste to scribble her name and number I wrote down her name as Yanna. She wasn't just another girl, another number in the night that comes and goes. I told Bobby, there's something here, this is going to be eternal not just temporal. A party doll she wasn't.

"Yeah, sure," was Bobby boy's flippant response, "Yeah, sure."

The weekend couldn't pass soon enough so I could call her at Good Samaritan Hospital where she worked. Monday finally arrived, and I was ebullient with romantic anticipation. Calling the number she had given me resulted in the voice on the other end indicating that no Yanna worked there. My hot to trot heart took a nose dive. She stiffed me, I thought to myself. But before ending the call, and in one last act of desperation, I asked if there was a girl there with a name that sounds close to Yanna. "Who is this?" the anonymous female voice at the other end responded and "What do you want?"

I embarrassingly pleaded my case, telling her what had happened, and she responded, "A Yara works here. I'll put her on." Shortly the sexy mysterious voice from Friday night once again resonated in my ear, and my pulse quickened. Her name was as beautiful and mysterious and intriguing as she was. The pretty lady was majestic, and her personality was divine. She knew how to pierce a heart, and I was spirited away into her soul. We dated several times and she was as hot as a Bic lighter with a full flint.

Yara was pure class, and after three months I proposed and she accepted. I knew that night, blocking the sidewalk with my car, with Mr. Moon's romantic light, that heaven had sent me an angel. A chance meeting was not chance. I knew it then, and I know it now. She was sent by God, and I definitely got the better part of the deal.

I was as confirmed a bachelor as one can be and never figured myself for the marrying type. I knew I was only going to this party once, so we proceeded to throw a big bash at the Beverly Wilshire Hotel in Beverly Hills, and a bash it was. The wedding was as classy as she was.

Yara was born in Guadalajara, Mexico. Women born in Jalisco are called *tapatias*.

Her mother Rosalva, also a beautiful woman who in her younger years looked like Jean Harlow, brought Yara and her two older sisters and their grandmother to the United States when Yara was five years old. The single mother struggled and worked hard to provide for the girls. Their father had died soon after Yara was born. Her mother worked the fields near Tijuana while waiting for green card status. After legally immigrating she was able to find a job in a factory near downtown L.A. to provide for the family.

Yara was thrown into Catholic school in the first grade and spoke only Spanish. There was no E.S.L. program in the Fifties, so it was either learn English or fall by the wayside. The little girls from Mexico did what they had to do to survive just as their mother had done. A good Catholic education was essential in order for them to learn the ways of God and live by His commandments. Their mother was strict with them, and loving discipline was the law of the land in that house in Watts on East 70th. Street. The girls were raised to do the right thing and work hard to achieve a better life in a better country. The mother always stressed that a good education was the only way out of poverty. The caring and hard working mother never took a dime of public assistance. She made her own way in the land of opportunity, buying her first house in Watts – a neighborhood made up mostly of blacks and Hispanics. The woman embodied the goals, hopes, and aspirations of the American dream.

A cytotechnologist is one who studies and detects the deadly cells of cancer, like a cell detective. This was Yara's chosen career path. She was protecting and serving mankind through the eye of a microscope rather than my chosen path, through the barrel of a gun and a tin on my chest.

* * * * *

The sacrament of marriage is a covenant between a man and a woman, who form with each other an intimate communion of life and love founded and endowed with its own ordered nature by God. After several years as a police officer and living on the edge, both professionally and in my social life, I felt that something more was needed. Driving fast cars and chasing fast women seemed to work just fine up to now, but all of a sudden the bottle started looking half empty rather than half full. There had to be something or someone beyond just the physical or temporal of life's pleasures. A committed bond of love and commitment to the brunette with the name I never heard before lit the torch that until now I hadn't known I carried. Chapter 1 ended, chapter 2 had begun.

On February 25, 1978 at St. Paul the Apostle Church in the heart of Westwood, Yara and I declared our commitment and would be joined together until death would do us part.

St. Paul, the church's namesake, underwent a major conversion. He was a Jewish tax collector, named Saul, who vigorously persecuted Christians. He eventually became one of Christianity's strongest defenders and purveyors of the Word. I found the story of St. Paul to be one of the most inspiring and amazing in biblical history. Saul was on his way to Damascus to arrest and persecute Christians. On the road, just outside Damascus, a bright light engulfed him and he fell to the ground. A voice then spoke to him saying, "Saul, why do you persecute me?"

Saul answered, "Who art thou?"

The voice answered, "Jesus of Nazareth, whom you are persecuting."

Saul responded to the voice from heaven, "What shall I do, Lord?"

The Lord instructed him, "Get up and go into Damascus and there you shall be told of what you are destined for."

In just a few moments Saul's old life was shattered and remade into a new one. Saul was baptized into his new faith in Damascus, and after a hiatus in the Arabian Desert to reflect and prepare for his future work, he returned to Damascus and began preaching the Word. The Jews were enraged and plotted to kill him, but he escaped.

St. Paul established many churches and his Gospel writing and teachings have become a cornerstone of the Roman Catholic Faith. He was eventually arrested under the persecution of the Emperor Nero and beheaded. I was honored to also go through a conversion, and a new committed purpose in my life in God's house under the watchful eyes of St. Paul. Saint Paul, in one of his famous letters states, "Not in orgies or drunkenness, not in promiscuity and licentiousness, not in rivalry and jealousy, but put on the Lord Jesus Christ and make no provisions for the desires of the flesh."

In writing this book I contemplate on how this message would have resonated forty years ago at Woodstock or in today's pop culture. To say that I use the term "culture" loosely is an extreme understatement.

The lady "from Mexico with love" has stood by me for a remarkable 32 years, and, like a rare bottle of wine, gets better with age. She has taught me what unconditional love and humility are all about and how to place others before one's self. This was hard for me at first, but proved of great value later in life. As we danced to her favorite disco song by Tavares, Heaven Must Be Missing An Angel, in my heart I knew it definitely was.

HOLLYWOOD LAND -- IT'S DANGEROUS TO THE BODY, CORROSIVE TO THE SOUL

Life is like a ladder; every step we take is either up or down. – UNKNOWN

orrific screams bounced off the discolored walls of the vintage lobby, which greeted visitors to the old Hollywood police station, built in a renaissance revival style of the 1920's. The ragged relic sat on the east side of Wilcox Avenue just south of Sunset. Such notorious characters as Bugsy Segal had once sauntered through the double doors at its gateway. Characters always bounced in and out, but today they weren't notorious, just bizarre. Even worse than the scandalous screams bellowing from the tortured soul now standing before me was the severed ear which had once been plastered to the right side of his head. He than gently laid it down on the well worn mahogany desk top. His right hand was glued to his head; it was playing Hoover Dam restraining the Red River where the ear had once hung. Another crazed visitor poured in seconds behind him, also in melt down mode. "I love you, I'm sorry!" he loudly lamented. He was a big meaty guy with a brutish face. It wasn't hard to figure who played the feminine gender in this not so gay relationship. I bolted from behind the desk and grabbed his arms. He swung around and gave me a savage look, but before he could react the silver bracelets clamped down on a set of blood stained paws.

The police stations of the Los Angeles Police Department are geographic divisions with numbers as well as names. Hollywood Division was given the numerical number six and earned respect due to its age and historical significance. Old number six had seen too many glorious movie stars in inglorious moments over the past sixty years. If the yellowed nicotine stained walls could talk, what a story they would tell.

* * * * *

I smelled her before I saw her. A heavy dose of Jungle Gardenia perfume to rouse the animal instinct. She was a sinful siren in a dress full of desire. Her blouse was unbuttoned three or four buttons down from a slim tantalizing neck adorned by a string of pearls, which, if the real deal, had cost somebody plenty. What made the blouse even more appealing was that it was of the see-through variety. Her round rosy cheeks were part of a pretty face which had been visited by a little too much make up. The topping was auburn, cut short and neat. With her seductive smile and tight skirt she looked more appropriately dressed for a rendezvous at the dazzling disco rather than a trip to the local police station. That is of course, unless she was fishing for a lover or two that came safely wrapped in a dark shade of blue.

She shook my hand in a strong masculine grip that spoke self-assured confidence. Her soft brown eyes met mine a little longer than they had to before she spoke, "I'm Carla", she said softly, then added, "the breather" as she leaned closer over the old mahogany desk. A friendly feminine voice had been making obscene phone calls to the Hollywood Police Station on-and-off for months. In addition to other desired effects she had aroused the curiosity of the "victim" cops.

So this was the mystery woman attached to the vivacious voice. She was as salacious in the flesh as she was on the phone. Carla paused for a long breath to let it sink in and then added, "I love cops, love sex, and my husband isn't enough." She held up a well manicured hand with a dazzling diamond chunker that screamed married. "No involvements, just sex," she stated matter-of-factly. Carla then handed me a list of some of the cops who she got to know telephonically and asked if they were in the station so she could meet them.

* * * * *

That's the way it went at old number six in Hollywood. It was often said that even the normal people in Hollywood division weren't normal.

An old Hollywood actress from the silent screen era would call the station daily to get radiation readings emitted from flying saucers from Mars that buzzed her Art Deco mansion off Laurel Canyon. New unsuspecting officers would actually take her seriously, and the rest of us would break out in mocking laughter. This went on for years. One officer even created a radiation machine complete with a dial and while on patrol would courteously stop at her house, have a cup of coffee with her, and provide the radiation reading in person. She too loved the police, but with her, the love stopped with the coffee, and any jolt derived was from caffeine.

That's how it went at the Hollywood division. Some of the cops in Hollywoodland, which was also referred to as Disneyland for adults, were as goofy as those they protected and served. A disgruntled young cop had an adversarial relationship with one very contentious captain. At a Christmas party on the Queen Mary one year, the cop and captain collided in a colossal collision of marvelous mayhem. In true slapstick style the cop hired a prostitute to throw a pie in the captain's face. The humiliated and overwrought captain was so stunned that the prancing prostitute made a clean getaway.

* * * * *

Hollywoodland seemed to be a Dante's Inferno on steroids, drugs, sex, whores, pimps, runaways, rapists, robbers, dope fiends, and enough goofies to fill a year-round Disney cartoon. Some sold out for money, some sold out for honey.

Unbelievable isolation seemed to attach itself to all these lost losers. Maybe it was too much smog, or elusive illusions. Hollywood was like a big lost-and-found with the emphasis on lost and very little found, except trouble. A few stepped back out of the darkness, but fire consumed the rest. Sooner or later, dead or alive, they would come in contact with the blue suitors with the badge. We were the ring leaders of this circus of fools and the greatest show on earth.

In the movie Wall Street the Michael Douglas character establishes the cogent conviction that to be successful one had to think outside the box. Police work is no different.

"Six Adam One, Six-A-One, a four-fifteen woman with a knife, Hollywood and Western code two," the Motorola radio screamed out. It was a full moon that hot, sticky July evening, and loons and lunatics would pour out into the Hollywood night as if answering some demonic call when the full moon danced bright. The fifty-plus disheveled woman felt annoyed, crummy, and alone. She grabbed a steak knife and decided to threaten the world. As I turned on to Western from Hollywood a crowd had already gathered, and a TV news truck from KTLA had just bounced to the curb. A petite female newscaster with a crooked smile, who looked better on the box than in person, had her "Breaking News" lead for tonight's show.

Two foot-beat cops were already code 6 there, but they had had no luck in getting her to cancel her dance of derangement and drop the knife. As my partner and I approached the dizzy damsel, she was babbling about lethal lasers from flying saucers that were trying to strike her dead. Either it was the full moon or she skipped her meds along with dinner, whatever. A knife is considered a deadly weapon and my partner drew his gun ordering her to drop the knife as she advanced. The infamous "Eula Love" shooting from a couple of years earlier, where two L.A. cops emptied their revolvers into a menacing madam with a knife, flashed big in my brain. The headlines read, "LAPD Guns Down Upset Woman Over Unpaid Gas Bill." I was determined that this would not be a deadly replay.

I calmly approached her and asked, "Do you know why my police car has white doors and a white roof, darling?" She looked puzzled at first, and then flattered that I had called her "darling." It had been many moons since she was somebody's darling.

"Why?" she asked cautiously.

"The white reflects the lasers from the saucer. If you get in the car you're safe, but first you have to put down the knife."

She threw down the knife and ran for the car, throwing herself in head first. The crowd cheered and the petite news reporter with the crooked smile had a story with a happy ending.

* * * * *

Tyrone Tyler and Luther Lamont were washouts, small time thugs who were waiting for the big score that never came, but needed some coin for happy rocks (crack cocaine). Radio traffic on the Motorola came to a dead stop followed by the adrenaline producing three loud beeps that patrol cops lived for, "All units in the vicinity and Six-A-One. Six-A-One, a two-eleven in progress of a yellow cab north Fuller between Sunset and Santa Monica, handle code three."

I was car commander that day, working with a young copper named Bobby Bascom who was riding shotgun. We looked at each other in disbelief. We were right around the block. I floored the big hulking AMC Matador of "Adam 12" fame, and after two two-wheel turns spotted the cab. The driver was cradling his bloodied forehead. He pointed into the back end of a parking lot. The robbers were in full gallop, and we were some forty yards behind. It was cops and robbers Hollywood-style. A thick heavy chain hung long and low between two poles buried in concrete. On foot they would have lost us. I yelled to Bobby, "Make sure your belt is on. We're gonna go for it." Heel and toe floored the black-'n-white with all 401 cubic inches roaring to life. Thirty-nine hundred pounds of Detroit iron lunged at the ring of steel snapping it like a clothes line. As contact was made, the charging Matador's grill flew from its resting place between dual sets of headlights that would never cast a sheen again. Fenders and tires collided in horrific screeching friction. Thug one and thug two dove under a mass of parked vehicles and went into a low crawl. I saw the gun, and it saw me, but I had the drop on him, and I guess he didn't feel lucky. Tyrone and Luther were taken into custody, and the two two-time losers hit the big three and struck out. I wiped my sweating brow and we high-fived each other as the cavalry arrived. The Matador sat bruised and battered. Coolant oozed onto the hot mill (the engine) producing steam above and green slime below.

I made eye contact with Bobby and let go with a fast, "We didn't see the chain. It was an accident."

Bobby smiled and responded with a quick, "Got it."

An accident is an unintentional occurrence and therefore unavoidable. My penance would have been stronger if the ramming were seen as deliberate. A traffic safety board would probably have given me days off. Bobby and I got a commendation, and I also got a reprimand. In LAPD lingo that means "you done good boy, but don't do it again."

* * * * *

Prostitution and its associated street robberies were a big problem on my beat and the subject of many complaints. Hookers on Sunset, pretty boys on Santa Monica Blvd., and the "dragons" (drag queens) who frequented Hollywood Blvd. usually came out at night. They were too stoned during the day to even have sex. Businessmen, who were in need of a lunch time quickie, could find happiness at the All-American Burger joint on Sunset. A guy could get a burger on the bun and/or a pair of flesh filled buns. It was one stop shopping and both were juicy.

To foul the plugs of prostitution and narcotic activity, I would curb my black-'n-white in front of the burger stand with the yellow caution lights blinking bright and sit to join the girls with some witty banter. "Come on DiPaola you're screwing up business," they would good-naturedly admonish me. Good police work involves good informants, and the "ladies" were as good as it got. They provided valuable dope-dealing info, and I let up on the heat. The cat came, and the mice melted away. The "johns," too, got hip to the heat and would find some place else to get happy. A profound sense of humor is an essential part of police work. To add to the fun and frolic I would play a cassette of the song, "I Fought the Law and the Law Won," over the car's P.A. system as I left. This would also spook the drug dealers at Hollywood and Western.

Hollywoodland was a bizarre cesspool of immorality where vice trumped virtue. It was home to just about every insidious and perverted act known to man, and then some. From "chicken hawks" who hung tight at the Gold Cup, a ptomaine restaurant at Hollywood and Las Palmas trolling for teenage boys, to Miss Mickey the dominatrix. The city of dreams to some was the city of dread to others. Some were sex hungry predators, some were just sex hungry.

When smog took a breather, the Hollywood hills came into view. They were dotted with a variety of structures people called home. They ranged from A-frames, heavy in the glass department, to the large palatial abodes with the proverbial terra cotta roofs and wrought iron gates. The gates protected trophy wives and pools filled with sun bathing beauties. The circular driveways were overflowing with Beamers and Benzes.

Some things belonged in the Hollywood hills, and some didn't. One of those things that didn't was a dead body. The black-'n-white churned up the hill, and just off the road there she was: lifeless, naked, and dead – very dead and painfully pallid. She looked like a Macy's mannequin between fittings. The discarded damsel had probably been killed by the Hillside strangler, and I secured the scene until Robbery-Homicide Division arrived. An unmarked light green Plymouth pulled in behind the black-'n-white. I immediately became transfixed on the Fedora hat attached to the graying head of Robbery-Homicide's oldest and most elite detective. He was the last of the remaining infamous LAPD Hat Squad. He was the best of the best, and as a young policeman I was in awe. It was a tremendous honor to meet this man. I gave him a cursory salute and a quick explanation of the murder scene.

He let go with a respectful smile and said, "Son, police work was a lot easier in my day than it is for you guys today."

I made with a quick, "How's that sir?"

"In the old days we didn't have to worry about reading anybody their rights; imagine the stupidity of telling somebody they don't have to talk to you. Getting a confession was relatively simple," he said.

"How's that?" I responded again.

"My partner and I would take a suspect up to the tallest building in L.A., which at the time was that building on your badge, City Hall. He would pick the suspect up by his ankles and dangle him over the edge while I took out my field officer's notebook taking copious notes of his responses to my partner's questions. Within three to five minutes we had everything we needed to know." We both smiled and I assisted this living LAPD legend in his investigation.

* * * * *

Screaming men calls were a common radio call on Friday and Saturday nights at a dive apartment building on Ivar, just south of the Boulevard. Miss Mickey, of dominatrix fame, entertained her gentlemen callers in a second floor studio outfitted in the usual black lingerie and black boots that bondage-seeking customers loved. The walls were naughty noir and provided a home for every type of physical restraint imaginable. Miss Mickey was a true capitalist who provided service with a smile to those in need of a little friendly S&M. She was so creative she could even provide an erotic use for a slinky.

Miss Mickey made her living from first class fools who wanted to walk on the wild side. The dimly-lit dump was a pleasure palace of perversity. The debonair dominatrix was really a nice Italian girl from Brooklyn named Mickey Martini, who had a compelling urge to stop being nice. Since her den of pleasure and pain wasn't conspicuous or complained of, it wasn't a priority for the short-handed and overwhelmed Hollywood Vice Unit.

When not in testosterone titillating attire and in soft clothes, Mickey Martini looked wholesome enough to be taken home to mother as a prospect for wedded bliss. Working the Hollywood foot beat (FB 2) gave me the opportunity to lean on the curvaceous cookie and get creative with my investigative techniques. Most of her customers were married, so I placed friendly phone calls to a few too unsuspecting and unhappy wives about their spouse's recreational routines. A very mad Mickey Martini stormed the station with her Beverly Hills lawyer in toe to "beef" me big time for harassment. It didn't go anywhere, but the bosses told me to lay off and leave it to Vice. They would get to it eventually.

I almost went along, but then it got personal. She teamed up with a pernicious pimp named Willy Watson. Her new boyfriend, a real gangster of love, also called Sweet Caddie Daddy by some of his other squeezes, cut her in on some of his dope action. She was hooked. Sweet Caddie Daddy also let it drop that he was tight with some patrol cops and wouldn't get busted. That's where the personal part came in. If he slithered instead of walked, a fine ruthless reptile he would have made.

Hell was licking its chops at devouring the tempting soul of Mickey Martini. Willy had a propensity for making plush tramps out of men wanting woman. Mr. Willy learned his pimping and pandering routine from eyeballing too many Superfly flicks. The pretty Italian girl from Brooklyn added a dose of class and diverse perversity, which increased his roll of pocket green. It also didn't hurt his living-legend pimp persona. She started branching out to the high-end hotel trade, and Willy provided the back-up and protection from other pimps or treacherous tricks that got out of line. Sweet Caddy Daddy paraded his new hot Italian dish around town in his ostentatious white over white Fleetwood Brougham. Willy baby seemed to have a thing for the color white, whether it had two legs or four wheels.

I was on Willy like a cheap suit. He became so well-trained that when he saw my black-'n-white he would pull over even before the flashing reds lit him up. The Brougham became a familiar sight at the Holiday Inn on Highland and other Hollywoodland hotels. Maybe it was that we were both from Brooklyn, but I was determined to save Miss Mickey from herself and the eventual fate of going back to Brooklyn in a box. Or perhaps it was my profound sense of chivalry, coupled with an intense dislike for bad-ass pimps who did in dolls and dead-ended their dreams.

Finally Miss Mickey gave me the opportunity I needed. She was still using her New York drivers' license with no picture, and I never positively confirmed her identity. A well-placed phone call to her mama and papa from the Los Angeles Police Department, conducting a vice investigation, did the trick. Mama emotionally confirmed her daughter's identity, but thought her daughter was working as a secretary. When she told Papa Martini, he was so upset he had a heart attack. The next day Miss Mickey stormed in to the station in maniac mode. I never heard my name laced with so many profanities. The guys at the station now referred to her as the "Mad Martini," and put signs up in the station house advertising a new Frank DiPaola cocktail called the "Mad Martini."

No complaint was taken, because the m.o. was legit. Presumably Miss Mickey went back where she came from to help take care of Papa, and started a new life. Her love shop went dark, and we never saw her again. Sweet Caddy Daddy had to find himself another ivory-skinned Hollywood squeeze, and he too left town due to a heavy dose of black-'n-white fever. Word on the street was that the "Mad Martini" got married back in Brooklyn. The happy hubby would forever believe that his beautiful bride was the wholesome honey he believed her to be.

* * * * *

The bosses had it figured that, for a patrol cop, I spent too much time chasing whores, pimps, and dope dealers. "Sooner or later you're gonna get your tit in a ringer," the brass warned. They liked my fine felony recap but the commendable cop capers sometimes danced a little too dangerous. A perfect example was Benny Bunz. I hit the reds on Benny's bashed-in Buick because one of his tail lights had lost their glow. Benny was usually good for a dime bag or two, but this time all he had was a joint which temporarily called the back of his ear home.

Benny also forgot his driver's license that moon-lit evening, so the Buick was up for grabs to be impounded. Under the glow of the black-'n-white's flashing party hats we played "Let's make a deal." He accompanied me to the station and ordered up a quantity of dope from his supplier while I listened in. I then got a telephonic search warrant for the dopey dope dealer and Benny got to enjoy a few more Hollywood nights.

Benny buys in, and off we go. The joint loses its resting place and meets boulevard black top in a crushing underfoot blow. Sergeant "stab-in the back" Stewart reluctantly agrees to my spontaneous narco caper. "Stab in the back" got his name from conducting quality control audits from individuals that officers had initiated contact with. This was for the purpose of soliciting complaints.

He also would follow officers around on patrol, hoping to burn them for not wearing their covers (hats), or for parking the black-'n-white on the wrong side of the street. Once I had the warrant teletype from the D.A.'s office he didn't have much choice. The good Sarge then approved another unit for back up. We parked the black-

'n-whites around the block from the dealer's house. I took off my uniform shirt and gun belt, slid my two inch backup revolver in a side pocket, and went to the door.

I made with a low knock and dopey asked, "Who is it?"

"Frankie D, Benny's cousin," I said.

Clyde opened the door and cordially began the conversation with, "Let's see your green."

He had dozens of baggies packaged for sale in plain view. I pulled the revolver on him, and his eyes turned to ice. Once he was cutely cuffed I played house with the friend of Benny Bunz and was the Shell answer man for his calling customers who were placing to-go orders. Nobody ever got plugged into my uniform pants and black military type spit-shined paw covers. They were all as dumb as he was and fell for that stupid "I'm Clyde's cousin" routine. After three more arrests plus Clyde, we were ready to pack it in.

In a back bedroom we found a machine for making phony credit cards and blank cards ready to have names imprinted. Bunco-Forgery Division was called in to handle the investigation and we scored four felonies and twelve hours overtime. Not everybody was happy. Sergeant "stab-in-the–back" Stuart had a "come to Jesus" meeting with me: "Yeah, it was a good caper, and you upped the felony recap, but we were behind on radio calls all day because two units were out of the field. You're not in dope anymore, so just handle your area." I did it my way. I was trying to boil the ocean. Now I would do it their way, maybe.

My old buddy Demetri had transferred into Hollywood about a year earlier. He got tired of being a ghetto gunfighter in the south end. Demetri had built up quite a reputation as one hell of a street cop, but things didn't sail smooth for long. LAPD has a reputation for "eating its own," and Demetri's head was on the plate. Two of his partners on the morning watch got jammed up in a criminal beef and started dimming off other cops so they could cut a deal. Demetri was one of those other cops who got the bum's rush. Integrity was Demetri's middle name. He wasn't just a good cop, he was a great cop. In typical LAPD fashion, you're guilty until proven innocent. Demetri was sucker-punched by the "guilt by association fist" of some foaming at the mouth I.A. head hunters.

Internal Affairs is a fast track to promotions, and sometimes the suits get overzealous.

Demetri had his discouraging day in court and was arraigned at the criminal courts building at 210 West Temple Street. There is no worse blow to a police officer than to be arrested, booked, and to be a defendant in a court of law. The tables had been turned on my good friend. To give him moral support I went up to him in open court, shook his hand, and with heart felt sadness offered, "I know you're innocent, I'm with you brother."

The I.A. squints that surrounded Demetri were bubbling over with arrogance and self importance. They were all wearing the same cheap suits that came off a J.C. Penney close-out sale rack. Maybe they got the group discount. They gave me the "you're a scumbag" look of disgust, and for the first time in my LAPD career I was not proud of the LAPD. The Department had acted way too quickly to go after Demetri, and the other officers who worked with the rogue cops. The word was that the department was on a witch hunt. If they want you bad enough they will find something.

Not even an hour passed since my court room bonding session with Zorba the Greek, that I was the subject of a come to Jesus meeting again, to end all come to Jesus meetings. News of the Italian-Greek love fest must have started a slow burn through the hallowed hallways of Parker Center and beyond. I was out for the count before I even entered the ring. Lt. Mike Malone, a.k.a. "Mike the Machete," was anxiously awaiting my arrival back at the station. I did a slow climb up the stairs to his office and made with a reluctant knock. Stepping through the door his eyes met mine. I knew I wasn't going to be the flavor of the month. The "machete" always had somewhat of a crazed angry look, except today it was like a double shot of crazed and angry.

Lt. M&M, as he was also referred to, had a glaze under his eyelids which shot out at me like a laser. His tight lips formed a thin line, definitely not a happy face. I knew this would be the afternoon to end all afternoons, only matched in dread by the time I got the axe from the police academy. The temperature immediately rose to Fahrenheit 150 degrees when I walked through the door. By nature he was cocky and insolent with the personality of a sweat sock. He had a rubber stamp for meanness. His voice was hard and pernicious with that "don't fool with me" tone. He was the hatchet man for the captain, who never soiled his lily white golfing hands. The thin face with the grizzled look was hard and mean. Before we broke bad the conversation went something like this.

"You're either stupid or a disloyal officer. What were you doing glad-handing a crooked cop in open court? I. A. gave me a full report. It's right here. I checked to see if you were on city time; you weren't. You didn't use a city car, so I can't burn you for that either. Now what do you have to say for yourself?" he demanded.

My eyes were angry and intense as I made with a quick sarcastic reply. "Lieutenant, all due respect, but I thought in this country we were innocent until proven guilty."

"You know the Department doesn't railroad people. Of course he's guilty," M&M shot back at me.

"Lieutenant, wouldn't you stand by a friend in need when the going got tough?" I asked.

He disregarded the question and fired back, "You don't get it, DiPaola. You are siding with a rogue cop, and your disloyalty could cost you if you don't apologize and ask forgiveness. Future promotions could be on the line."

Talking to the "machete" was like having a conversation with a hub cap. We were going 'round and 'round and getting nowhere. We engaged in some more of this chit chat, and he kept playing the same record. Even though my head was on the chopping block, the listening stopped.

I stood up and offered, "Lieutenant, I think I'm wasting your time, may I leave now?"

He jabbed back, "You don't seem much impressed by the situation you are in."

I returned the jab, "I did what I had to do, Lieutenant."

Again he reiterated, "This could affect your future with the Department."

I was jousting on a solid argument based on conviction, but M&M was playing the party line. I gave him a cursory, "Thank you, sir," did an about face, and left the office without even shaking the hand of the "machete." His words cut like a knife and I experienced first hand why he was called "Mike the Machete." The basically one-way disheartening discourse had a pernicious effect on my already somber spirit.

* * * * *

Most cops are naturally die-hard cynics, and I swore that I would never become like them, but I did. We were all idealists for the first few years on the job until the cynical reality finally tumbled in, not only from the streets, but from within. Depression took control of my soul and vigor. Constant negativity was turning me inside out. A cop needs a sense of humor and a coat of armor to keep the crap from penetrating and to survive. Both of mine were rapidly retreating.

Funny situations were becoming aggravating, and suspects I arrested often didn't stay arrested. While there were some successes, the futility of it all was heaving heavy. Hard-charging cops were constantly building up beefs. The more arrests, the greater the chance things would go sideways. We didn't get a commission, just personal satisfaction for soliciting guests to the downtown gray-bar hotel. The pay check was the same whether you hustled or just cruised. No wonder so many cops married the bottle or took a one-way trip, compliments of Mr. Smith and Mr. Wesson. I was being eaten by the monster of malignant malaise. Maybe "Mike the Machete" did me a solid. I would have to find a new home.

Zorba the Greek ended up being the protagonist in his own Greek tragedy. When it came down to it, the stand-up guy stood alone. The big Greek was eventually acquitted of all charges. This means that it basically never happened. Charges were dismissed with a jury impaneled, and they can never be refilled. The humiliation and malevolent stigma would always hang heavy. Demetri's ship had been forever sunk. The copper's copper would cop no more, and I was slowly getting the same sinking feeling, but the summer of my discontent wasn't over.

My last day in Hollywood Division was not a happy one. Tiny Naylor's, the nostalgic drive-in that once called Sunset and La Brea home, would be my last Hollywood hurrah. My partner and I were enjoying our complimentary cup of coffee when the comely car-hop leaned into the open window of our black-'n-white. She indicated that a contentious customer refused to pay up and wouldn't leave. Eager to help a damsel in distress we obliged. The suspect was too many inches over the six foot mark with a build that spoke prison. As we approached he stood up gracefully, like a panther that was about to attack. His dark eyes gave me a morose steady glare.

Sense number six told me I should have either called in sick that day, or gone to another pop spot for a cup of hot and black. I told him to step outside and he reluctantly complied. He was a big man whose gait was slow and deliberate. The giant looked like he could have gone a few rounds with King Kong and come out on top. He was the strong silent type all right, totally non-communicative. My questions were met by sounds of silence. His dark skin was sweating. The eyes that met mine had horizontal and vertical nystagmus. I had him figured for a duster (someone under the influence of the animal tranquilizer PCP or phencyclidine). I figured right. As my partner and I went to cuff the not so jolly giant, every bone and muscle in his body pulled rigid. The panther turned and struck my partner with a body blow that made him tumble down like London Bridge. I sprang up to place a choke hold, but he flipped me over his body. He was trying to get my partner's gun so I again tackled him. The tangled up mass of black and blue rolling around in the parking lot provided show time entertainment for the lunch crowd.

I used every baton move that the good Sergeant McMuscle ever taught, but with each jab the moose got madder. Blood poured from his head, but like a wounded bull he kept coming. I was in pretty good shape in those days, but three to four minutes of all out fighting can make a body tired. It seemed like an eternity. We were in a death fight to the finish. Our options were running out. On the escalation of force barometer, it was voice commands first, pain compliance second, baton third, and then Mr. Smith and Mr. Wesson. Our batons had rolled away and my partner had taken such a pummeling he was almost out and trying to stop the blood where the gorilla from hell had bitten him. In desperation I tackled him again going for the neck. This time he threw me with such ferocity that I landed six feet from the initial point of contact; my flesh and bone collided violently with ground zero. In an attempt to break the free fall I landed on my right wrist (my gun hand), which went snap, crackle, and pop. By this time the crowd was selling tickets. A sympathizing hooker who figured she owed me one, grabbed the mike from its dashboard resting place in the black-'n-white, and requested help. These were the days before 911 calls and cell phones. The cuddly car-hop had called Hollywood desk and got the proverbial busy signal. I awkwardly pulled my gun with my left hand from the Bianchi breakfront, and with what little strength was left pointed it at Godzilla. Sounds of sirens filled the noon-time air and I let go with a mumbled, "thank God." Godzilla got down on his knees and started crying.

It took half the day watch to hook and book Godzilla that sunny afternoon in happy Hollywoodland. I never did get to finish that delicious cup of hot and black, and as far as Hollywood was concerned I was on the transfer and never went back. I don't know what it was about the city of Satan that seemed to make people's problems so dramatic, but if the soul were to designate a destination for agony it would be the checker board of untruths; Hollywoodland. I left with my right arm in a cast and my soul in a hole. It's like I said in the beginning; "Dangerous to the body, corrosive to the soul."

DETECTIVE HEADQUARTERS

I stick my neck out for nobody.
— FROM *CASABLANCA*

etective Lieutenant J.P. Jackson took a long puff on a well-worn Macanudo as his eyes laconically bounced from my plaster encased forearm to my penetrating baby browns.

Eyeballing my cast he humorously offered up, "What did the suspect look like?"

"Fourteen stitches to the head and a return ticket to Folsom for being a bad boy on parole," I replied.

"I'm Lieutenant Jackson, but due to a big-time lack of respect around here everybody calls me J-P. Do you smoke stogies, officer?" J-P asked in a manner halfway between fact-finding and sarcastic. He was trying to feel me out.

"Maduros," rolled off my tongue as we sized each other up.

J-P was a big, bulky guy with a receding hair line, but still enough of the white stuff left to run a comb through. His collar was unbuttoned, and the paisley tie looked like an afterthought. The tops of white sox that matched his hair snuck up from a pair of cowboy boots that could have been worn by Hopalong Cassidy.

"Most of us here are just doing our time, kind of like a paid sabbatical from cops and robbers stuff. So do your job but don't get too happy. We don't like stress or writing paper; it makes us light-headed. My only pet peeve is that you need to show up on time. And with that glorious introduction, welcome to DHD," J-P said.

J-P's lips broke with a smile and a vise grip-like hand shake which let me know that he was the stuff real cops are made of, and crossing him wouldn't be in my best interest.

"Now for your first assignment, since you're Italian, you got any connections to some good wop food?" the good Lieutenant gastronomically asked with a smile.

"I can handle the smokes and the eats lieutenant, I mean J-P" I responded with a self-assured smile.

J-P was testing me to see if I would fit in with the good old boys; the holdover dinosaurs of the past. LAPD was changing, as was the rest of the world. As the 1980's were ushered in, the old school coppers were determined to hold onto antiquity as long as they could. I kept J-P in pocket with hand-rolled stogies from a cop-friendly tobacco pop spot on the south end of Main, and half-price pasta and Parmesan dinners from Palermo's on Vermont near Franklin.

Detective Headquarters was a final resting place for worn out warriors whose end game was a pension and fun in the sun. DHD was basically command central for LAPD on weekends and after hours for any occurrence bigger than a parking ticket.

I took telephonic notifications and dished out advice to field cops on criminal issues. Veteran detectives also boned me up on the finer points of death investigations. It was our responsibility to determine the causes of death. When I wasn't playing secretary with a gun, or diagnosing dead bodies, newspaper reading and an official office TV set kept me happy. The hours on pm's (from 3-11:30) did a slow crawl. The high point of the evening was the eleven o'clock news which ushered in the final thirty minutes of the watch.

It was the beginning of the end. I was where I wanted to be. Like Bogey in "Casablanca," I didn't have to stick my neck out for nobody. An occasional "decomp" or "stinker" (a body that had been dead too long) was about the only unpleasantness a DHD copper had to endure. At least they don't try to beat you, beef you, or sue you. I loved DHD.

* * * * *

Brain matter mingled with blood and chunks of flesh (that were once part of somebody's face) found a home on a fine feminine wardrobe emblazoned with Christian Dior and Givenchy labels. The high-dollar rags must have cost somebody plenty. That somebody in life was Dr. George Goody, whose name definitely bore no resemblance to the picture before me. Apparently the good Doctor Goody grew tired of being cuckolded by a cunning and conniving wife. So he decided to show her a thing or two, in not so living color. He blew his brains out, or so it appeared, in her Plaza- suite like clothes closet. A heavy dose of ruby red pigmentation added to an elegant wardrobe that was elegant no more.

It was hard to discern if the mourning missus was distraught from the death of her once-upon-a-time hubby or the destroyed once-glittering garments. Maybe she did it, maybe the boyfriend, or the butler did it. There was a mine field full of maybes, or just maybe it was what it appeared to be, suicide. This was one of my first "K" car capers at DHD, as Detective Headquarters Division was referred to. It was up to me to get cozy with a conclusion. The "K" car should have had a "D" designation since those detectives were assigned to handle death investigations, and the puzzle of determining if the cause of death was a murder, natural, or suicide. The "K" stood for king, which was the radio designation for DHD. (You needed to know that, right?)

In the old film noir Who-Done-It?'s of the 30's and 40's, wanton wives and their lovers always conspired to do in the hapless husband by making it look like an accident or suicide. The movie classic "Double Indemnity" flashed big in the nostalgia retention room of my brain as I entered a bedroom that was bigger than a basket ball court. The stately colonial stood just off Los Feliz Boulevard and smelled of money. It was the kind of place you would expect a doctor or uptown big shot to own. The lady in tears who greeted me wasn't exactly Barbara Stanwyck. A few too many years and the wrinkles that went with them helped her lose that cover girl complexion of youth and yesteryear. She was still attractive, though, in a mature sort of way.

Her husband's head, or what was left of it, had all the signs of a suicide. A contact shot at the base of the temple where the revolver's muzzle was pressed. The visible damage caused by a contact shot is due more to the flame and expanding gases than by the penetration of the bullet itself. If the gun had been between two and eighteen inches, the tell-tale signs of smudging (a deposit of smoke and soot from the burned powder around the entrance wound), and tattooing (unburned powder residue and minute molten metal particles driven under the skin) would have been present if a homicide. Besides, few murderers would hold a gun directly in contact with someone's head. It would be too messy. I gave the missus a gunshot residue analysis test (GSA), and she came up clean. Homicide Division concurred, and the case was cleared as a suicide.

* * * * *

As I entered the apartment on North Bronson I gave it a quick visual and was amazed at how neat and tidy the place was for a bachelor pad. The middle-aged corpse, who that morning would have been described as a middle-aged man, hadn't been dead too long. Rigor mortis (a stiffening of the muscles as a result of chemical changes in the body after death) hadn't crept in yet. Rigor mortis usually develops first in the face and neck in the first few hours of death, followed by the upper torso, and then moves south. In life his name had been Randall. I guess it still was. When Randall decided to check out he chose to be as meticulous about his death as he was about his life. He lay down on the couch and placed his wrist over a plastic trash bag which he most carefully laid out between the coffee table and the couch. The bag was strategically placed to capture the red river blood flow from the split vein from which it would never again flow. Randall's fastidious phobia for neatness was overwhelming, since he lived alone. Most suicidal types are usually so distraught that their concern for the cleaning crew doesn't enter in the big play. Randall died as he had lived, neat and all alone.

Carl was the second db (dead body) that night. He looked like a surfer dude whose blonde hair had seen too much sun. His eyes were wide open. Sitting on the floor with his legs crossed and his back against the couch, he didn't look dead, but was. A blue steel thirty-eight lay at his side. When the skin is stretched by a bullet during entry, the entrance wound appears smaller than the diameter of the bullet. Bleeding at the entrance wound is only a small amount, and tissue destruction is not too great at that point. I couldn't initially see the entrance wound, but when I examined the back of his head, I got the big picture. When a bullet passes through the body it packs tissue or brain matter in front of it and causes a larger and a more ragged, torn hole going out than where it went in. The surfer dude died with a smile on his face. As I looked into the open eyes of death that morbidly met mine, a biblical passage came to mind, "You have given light to their eyes that they shall not sleep in death." I hoped he believed.

* * * * *

The attic of the porno theater on Western Avenue was cramped and as hot as the flicks they were showing. Maybe he was up there for a better view or just a place to sleep, but he wasn't asleep; he was dead. I smelled him before I saw him.

It was my second stogie, and it still couldn't extinguish the stench of death. When a person dies his blood pressure drops to zero, and the blood stops circulating. It then settles to the lowest point of the body and causes a purple discoloration, which is called post mortem lividity. This is useful in determining the time of death. Putrefaction is the growth of bacteria within the body, and after 24 hours decomposition begins. In police lingo this was a decomp, one that swelled, smelled, and turned brown. The five-foot tall coroner's deputy pleadingly asked if I could help her lift the bloated shell of a former life on to the gurney. I was about to give her the proverbial, "It's not my job," but my sense of chivalry kicked in. I grabbed his feet while she grabbed his shoulders, and we went into lift mode.

Big mistake. As we raised the bloated body, swelled from gaseous expansion, it burst like a balloon. The smell of death, which had all ready penetrated my mustache and nostrils, was joined by a splash of bodily fluids which had once been the sustenance of life. All the cigar smoke in the world would not negate death's explosive anger. Dealing with all this death definitely gave me a different perspective on life. The plain-wrapped ride (detective car) I piloted that day lit up several freeways getting home. I did a quick strip tease in the backyard and Yara hosed me down like a big dog. Even my German Shepard Dino (named after the Ferrari) kept a cool distance. My mustache and nose follicles had soaked up an overdose of death's nauseating nasal contaminating stink. It took several days, and dozens of nose baths, to rid myself of the deposits which had shot out from the exploding decomp.

* * * * *

The second floor apartment was in an upscale building on the west side. Mostly swinging singles and young professional couples – you might remember that they were called yuppies – called it home. The forty-something brunette may have been single, but she was no longer swinging. She was very naked and very cold. Her head lay comfortably on the pillow as if asleep. The vibrator was still in the "on" position doing what vibrators do, but now the intended affect rang hollow. The odor of death had not yet made the scene, and rigor mortis had not yet crept in.

"I hope she died happy," the patrol cop offered up.

This one was fresh, probably less than a couple of hours old. I unplugged the excitement machine before it did anymore damage and covered her. It was bad enough dying in the first place, but at least she should be allowed a little dignity. In Los Angeles County, if a deceased has been seen by a doctor within twenty days, he can sign off on the death certificate, and no autopsy is required. While waiting for the coroner, I found the doctor's name on a prescription bottle, and he was willing to sign off. Apparently she had a heart condition. As I looked at the face of contentment that would never again have a lustful longing, I shrugged my shoulders and let go with an almost silent, "Oh well." The only time I got beat up bad by dead bodies was when a child was involved. Somehow you have to learn to flick the little switch inside your head that handles emotion control to the 'off' position and hope it stays there.

* * * * *

When I wasn't cavorting with cadavers and trying to untangle the conundrum of their death and how they left the land of the living, the Los Angels Times, a rack full of car magazines, and even the spirituality of Thomas Aquinas helped the time crawl by. I made the chow run for the squad almost nightly, and J-P usually liked a little vino with his veal. What the hell, I thought, he was the boss and I was only following orders.

An ancient proverb says that, "Anybody who doesn't smile should not run a restaurant." Palermo's was on everybody's "A" list of tasty trattorias, especially the cops. Singing Sal was the proprietor, maitre d', chief cook, and bottle washer. He could dole out Italian love songs like a gondolier on a Venice canal. Sal loved making his customers happy, especially by offering them complimentary wine or espresso while they waited for a table. We were on duty, so we went for a petite cup of dago noir.

A three-piece Armani suit was definitely an improvement over my former uniform attire as a blue suitor. Pietro Berretta and a magazine full of nines hugged my waist. It was Italian all the way baby. The wop from "GQ," as my office cronies like to kid, was stylin'. Palermo's had such a good reputation with the cops that the parking lot was usually flooded with a sea of black-'n-whites. Word came down from the top that patrol coppers should be more diverse in their culinary habits. They should use greater discretion so the public wouldn't get the wrong idea, but it didn't help. Internal Affairs even paid Sal a not-so-courteous call advising him to charge cops full price instead of half. Sal threw them out, insisting that he could charge his friends whatever he wanted. Hooray for Sal! One for the cops, zero for Internal Affairs.

* * * * *

Among other things, DHD was where telephone calls got switched to; those calls that the rest of LAPD didn't know how to deal with or didn't want to know. One of those calls this particular evening had a voice attached to it by the name of Danny Delaney; specifically ex-cop Danny Delaney. Danny had been pensioned off after a debilitating on-duty traffic accident. The cop world is a world unto itself. Danny did not only miss the job, but the camaraderie and cop shop banter. He started calling almost nightly. Some of the guys would kiss him off when he called, especially when he and the "bottle" got a little too friendly.

Eventually he would only ask for me and we became telephone buddies. He insisted I call him Danny-boy, like his police pals used to at the station house, so I did. Danny-boy's wife had recently left him, and so did the companionship he desperately needed. Johnny Walker and Jack Daniels, along with too many packets of too many pain pills, replaced the wife and police pals of yesterday. When he needed station house blarney and reminiscing about war stories, it was me. Sometimes his mood made melancholy. He would talk about his funeral and how he wanted a chorus of cops to sing "Oh, Danny Boy!"

On this particular night Danny was definitely not making merry. Discontent, drugs, and desperation replaced what once consumed the conversation. Sense number six told me that this phone call would not have a happy ending; it was heading to a place neither one of us wanted to go. I motioned to my partner to get a trace going. Too many cops eat their guns like kids eat candy, except the results aren't sweet. I knew how he felt, sort of. Danny talked, or rather babbled, about being useless and not having a reason for living. He felt like a 9mm without a clip, just an empty shell. He had lost his cause and even blew it with his old lady.

Desperation dominated the phone call on both ends, and I started raising my voice into a very tense pitch. The squad room became smaller as concerned cops circled the wagons around my desk. Danny kept talking about the wake that he knew would soon descend on him like a black cloud, along with bagpipes and the ever present melodious "Oh Danny Boy!" He was no longer a cop, the man with the badge and all the answers. No longer the "go to guy." "Not only couldn't I keep my job, but everything else went South too", he sadly lamented.

I frantically looked up at Detective Ramos, who was still working the trace, but there was no high sign yet, just a forlorn frown and negative head shake. Listening to Danny brought back memories of Demetri. Now I really understood how the big Greek must have felt. So much about the past and Demetri; I had to get through to this guy before it was too late. He was on the edge of the river of no return. I was the only lifeline he had, and I hoped he would grab it. Trying to get him to give up the ghost took every ounce of energy and thought that I could muster. He wasn't listening.

The rambling monologue was like an express train which screamed by all the stops. All the frantic waving would not make it halt. Finally, the high sign from Ramos came. Danny was at a motel on Western Avenue, and units were rolling. Danny was barricaded behind a wall of despair and self-pity. I was banging, but the hammer wasn't breaking through. My head was glued to that damn phone. His voice became more and more distant and inaudible as it approached the eighty proof level.

Hope was taking leave of him, and I thought of my own loss and sense of purpose. The philosophy that: "I'm the only cause that I care about," didn't seem to cut it anymore. This guy was looking for the purpose-driven life he once had, and I was trying to sail fast and free. Maybe there was a reason Danny's wayward phone calls landed on my desk. Maybe this whole deadly fiasco was as much about me as it was about him. Detective Ramos, who everybody called the "preacher" because he was a deacon at his church, pulled out a set of rosary beads and brought a slow silent motion to his lips. I started yelling. I was in a panic mode, "Don't do it Danny, don't do it! You have everything to live for." My voice ran across town, they could even hear me in Santa Monica, I was yelling so loud.

"I gotta do what I gotta do. Thanks Frank."

"Oh Danny Boy, the pipes are calling from glen to glen and down the mountain side. The summer's gone and all the flowers are dying. Oh Danny Boy I love you so."

NORTH BY NORTHEAST- THE TWO DAGOS RIDE AGAIN

The only thing necessary for the triumph of evil is for good men to do nothing.
— EDMUND BURKE

t was a chance meeting in a southbound elevator at Parker Center that would give me a new purpose and a new beginning, on a road never traveled. The blotted box was filled to capacity – stuffed with detectives, civilians, and bodies in LAPD blue. They were all different sexes, sizes, shapes, and colors; a microcosm of L.A. itself and equally as crowded. Some were on their way to a bust and some bailing from one. The only thing I was on my way to was a down-home tuna melt soaked in grilled onions, surrounded by fiery jalapenos at a delightful dump across the street called the Kosher Burrito.

Among the boxed-in bodies, a pair of shiny new captain's bars attached to a blue suitor named Carl Covino caught my wandering eye. Carl and I had been probationers (rookies) together at "Shootin' Newton" a thousand years ago. We lost track of each other, but a heavy dose of fate and destiny must have been working overtime.

"Congratulations, Captain," I offer in surprise as our hands tightly gripped. Cops didn't hug each other in those days; it wasn't proper, and it might give someone the wrong idea. Captain Carl was on the fast track to LAPD stardom. His career was going up, and mine was traveling in the same direction as the elevator – down. Carl had borrowed my brand new three-piece suit for his first promotional interview at the beginning of his career, and it had worked.

"The suit that launched your career. If you need another one I've got a closet full now," I offered up with a smile. We both chuckled.

The elevator reached its destination, and we all spilled out in a mad dash to somewhere or nowhere. Captain Carl still seemed like the same right guy he'd always been. I was glad the rank and its usual accompanying ego inflation hadn't pressurized his persona into the ozone. Carl decided to join me for lunch and a visit to old times. He went for the greasy burger, and I fell for the coveted melted tuna surprise. What the heck, it was all good grease, but I talked myself into it that the tuna was the healthier of the two grease jobs. We caught up on life and his new command at the Northeast Division. Then came the second surprise, which had nothing to do with tuna. As I started to devour the second half of hot and greasy, Captain Carl invited me to transfer to Northeast and we would once again work together.

"You could work directly for me, and I will make it worth your while."

I guess he wanted to pay me back for the suit. Anyway, I was on my way to the next transfer and a new chapter with LAPD and 6045 York Boulevard, in the Highland Park section of Los Angeles, was my new career stop. Highland Park had once been predominately Italian and Irish, but now a majority of Hispanics call it home. Built in 1925, Northeast Division was also known as the Highland Park Police Station. It is now the oldest surviving police station in L.A. and definitely a throw back to another era. She was built in the renaissance revival style of the day. There was even a portico covering the driveway that led to the side entrance. This kept cops and cons alike from getting wet heads during one of the few times it did rain in sunny southern California.

The old Northeast Station is now the home of the LAPD Historical Museum. It has provided a real-life set for many a motion picture, including "Changeling," featuring Angelina Jolie directed by Clint Eastwood. The building was also the target of the Symbionese Liberation Army in 1974 with a bomb planted under its stately steps. Fortunately it fizzled before it could blow. The S.L.A. was better at kidnapping heiresses than bomb making.

Captain Carl slid easily into his news digs, and so did I. I filled in as his adjutant occasionally, and my new title was "Special Problems Coordinator." The special problems I was to solve mainly dealt with quality of life issues and community complaints. These included abandoned buildings and vehicles, drug dealing, prostitution complaints, and swarming, juvenile gang members congregating like bees waiting for a sucker to sting. My consummate analytical skills allowed me to coordinate the police resources to address community and business groups' concerns with the appropriate responses. This position was based on Professor James Q. Wilson's "Broken Windows Theory." If low level crimes and quality of life complaints go unaddressed, neighborhoods decline and the good people move out. This eventually leads to large-scale decay in these neighborhoods and spreads to other areas of the city. Little did I know that three years later my graffiti crackdown efforts would earn me a featured spot alongside Mr. Wilson on an ABC-TV prime time episode of "20/20."

As the newest member of the Highland Park Police, as the locals called us, Captain Carl greased my skids so that I worked days with weekends off. He also put the word out to pesky supervisors that I worked directly for him, so hands off. I was happy, the community was happy; it was a love fest.

Graffiti was becoming a real problem in L.A. in the late 80's and early 90's. The not-so-artful art was wearing thin on the good citizens of L.A. and was increasingly becoming a proverbial police problem. In days of old, graffiti was basically relegated to East L.A. and perpetuated by generational Hispanic gangs for the purposes of marking their turf. It also showed up occasionally in South Central L.A., perpetuated by black gangs for the same stupid reason.

That's all I really knew about graffiti, except for the fact that I didn't like it. It reminded me of a pimple or pock-marked face. No matter what kind of face you had, it got uglier with a dose of either one. Since part of my job was enhancing the community from the police side of the fence, I proposed to Captain Carl what I thought was a viable solution. I would take custody of juveniles arrested for graffiti, and, under police supervision, return them to the scene of the crime. There they would clean up their mess and learn the consequences of their actions. This would also send a message to the community that the police were serious about making their neighborhoods a better place in which to live.

The Captain bought off on the idea and suggested I find another copper to partner up with. He advised me to write up a proposal for our new unit, and he would make it happen.

Officer Donald DeLorenzo was a cop's cop who worked the front desk and was getting a heavy case of the burnout blues. I knew Don from my old ad-narc days. He transferred out of dope shortly after I rolled in. Don worked for Uncle Bernie, too, and had been quite an operator. Uncle Bernie would always lament, "I got rid of one dago and I get another one." Don was riding out his time as a Highland Park Police desk jockey until retirement or something better came along. Finally, it did; me!

Don was four inches south of the six-foot mark and had a happy face that was as round a Goodyear tire. With his black hair and swarthy complexion he could have easily called a pizzeria in Brooklyn home. He was originally from New York, too, but upstate – so it didn't count. Neither one of us fit the L.A. cop mold in either looks or persona, which is maybe why we clicked. We both liked doing things our way over the more rigid LAPD way. Supervisors, brass, and writing useless paper, just to make some pencil neck with a badge happy, were to be avoided.

I propositioned, and dago Don bit. He wasn't a people person. He didn't say much, because he didn't have to. Some called him dry, but it was more like insightful and sly. A week later we were in uniform in an alley supervising a bunch of pissed-off punks buffing out their own graffiti. My new partner was the proud father of five kids who were all straight arrow. You could tell he had a way with kids; authoritative yet patient and understanding. Personally, kids weren't my thing. With me it was about consequences and getting a pound of flesh. The knuckleheads played, now they paid. The Juvenile Impact Program was born then and there in that grimy, paint-splattered alley. Twenty years and ten thousand juveniles later (according to the LAPD website), it is still going strong.

The pounds of flesh I was trying to extract belonged to two Asian gangsters, yin and yang, along with two cholos (a slang term for a Hispanic gangster) named Chuey and Louie. There was an east-meets-west turf battle on the highways and byways of Highland Park, and these pee-wee gangsters got a little too happy with the spray paint.

"You play, you pay." I barked. "When you paint this crap out make it neat. Ten push-ups for every drop of paint that ends up where paint drops ain't supposed to be."

To get their rocks off and "diss" the Hispanics, yin and yang slipped into their rival's hood under cover of darkness. They "bombed" several alleys with a heavy Mandarin dose of not so ancient or flattering hieroglyphics. After a tense hour of fun in the sun, Chuey had a meltdown and got slaphappy with his fortune cookie friends. Don and I went into referee mode and broke it up before it got ugly. Chuey's last words before he was about to put Yang's lights out were Chino cabron (Mexican slang for "fucking Chinese").

He was a little light in the sensitivity department. I guess he must have skipped school on diversity day. Can't we all get along?

* * * * *

Once upon a time there was a diminutive damsel named Tanya Taylor. She was a single mom with a blonde blue-eyed ten-year-old son named Tommy Taylor. Tommy's nickname was "Tommy the Terrible." A name well-deserved. I know I'm dating myself, but he looked like the "Dennis the Menace" character played by Jay North in the Sixties TV show.

Tommy started stealing when he was eight, so by now he was a veteran. The final finale was when he cleaned out his mother's jewelry box and tried to unload the loot on unsuspecting classmates at school. He told them they would make great gifts for their mothers on Mother's Day. Not only was he a consummate thief, but his salesmanship skills weren't bad either. When confronted with his insidious behavior, Terrible Tommy threw terrible terror tantrums. Patrol cops received numerous radio calls to the Taylor home, and he was becoming a proverbial pain. On one of the radio calls a responding officer left a business card for the desperate mom to contact the two Dagos. It was an old story with a familiar twist: no daddy, no discipline, and Terrible Tommy was the result.

Now he would get discipline dago style. A visit to the old L.A. City Jail for a mock Scared Straight session tuned up the brazen brat and got his attention. Next we had to give our youngest enrollee a cause which he could excel at. He was too young for the graffiti paint-outs, so we assigned him the arduous task of washing police cars and spit shining their worn-out tires. After two weeks of this, Terrible Tommy was terrible no more, and the desperate damsel was desperate no more. Tommy started coming to the police station on a regular basis and now received the attention and discipline that he so desperately needed. Tanya Taylor got her life and her son back as the letter entitled "A Parent's Hope" so eloquently stated (see Appendix).

Due to a dearth of programs that actually had teeth and the results that go with them, the courts started referring to us any kid with the word trouble as his middle name. We received referrals for virtually every offense imaginable. Our galloping graffiti program caught the attention of the L.A. Times and the local TV news, which accompanied us on neighborhood paint-outs on several occasions.

"Police clean up the Southland with rookie gang members and taggers. Details at eleven," was one TV news headline. With all this hype the L.A. City Council and two local councilmen, whose districts were covered by the Northeast Division, also took notice. Captain Carl dragged me along to a community meeting, where he and councilmen Marty Melendez were the featured speakers.

An irate resident angrily asked, "What are you doing about all the gangs and graffiti?" The good councilman turned to yours truly and happily stated, "Officer DiPaola, who runs the Juvenile Impact Program, will be glad to answer your questions."

I wasn't even supposed to speak, so I shot from the hip with an answer. I briefly explained the program, then asked him where he lived.

"Off Hyperion near Sunset," he responded.

I shot from the hip again, but this time with both barrels. "Sir, I am very familiar with your area. You have an abandoned house where transients congregate, numerous abandoned vehicles, and more than a few drug dealers along with an overdose of graffiti. I'll be there this Saturday morning with some of the gang-bangers and taggers who are responsible for the graffiti. Not only will we paint out the entire neighborhood, but we'll clean up the area around the vacant house and run out the transients. In addition, I'll bring in the cavalry, and we will impound the abandoned vehicles and deal diligently with the drug dealers. I invite you and your neighbors to join us and participate if you like." I then turned to councilmen Melendez and extended an invitation.

To go a step further it was explained that we would contact the L.A. Building and Safety Department in an attempt to have the property declared a nuisance. Once the building was condemned, there was a possibility we could have the building demolished. Many of the one hundred or so residents in attendance applauded. Mighty Melendez gave me a double hand shake and thanked me for bailing him out.

The neighborhood clean up was a great success. By the end of that day the crew spilled sweat in buffing out over forty tagged premises. An assortment of not-so-happy drug dealers went to jail, and the tow yard added a few more impounds to their collection. In a bit of sarcastic irony, a few hesitant homies, tattooed in the same placasos as those on the walls, reluctantly volunteered to join the clean up, or else. A racy reporter from the local TV news went live with, "Police have even persuaded some of the local gang members to change their ways and help residents clean up their neighborhood." So a bit of irony and blarney bit big and beautiful that day. The contented councilman Melendez made a monetary donation to the program and gratuitously gave us our own graffiti vehicle. The cranky constituents were cranky no more.

When a youngster was referred to the program, the first step was an intake meeting with the offender and his parents. This enabled us to gain insight into the problem, make recommendations, and set ground rules. In some cases we were able to facilitate communication between the parents and kids. This helped solve the acrimony between them.

Youngsters were briefed in no uncertain terms on the rules of behavior and what would be expected of them. Like the patrol cars in our parking lot, our rules were black-'n-white. A major rule of ours was no long hair, earrings, or body-piercing. On one occasion a young man showed up with all of the above. "You are going to have to remove that stud and the hair tail has to go." I informed him. The young man adamantly refused, and the passive parents sided with their son. Dago Don went into over-drive explaining that they were guilty of the cardinal sin of "enabling" and making excuses for their son's behavior. We would have none of that here, and if their son did not comply with our rules, they could return to court and pay the fine.

Parents who enabled their offspring were all too typical. They wanted to be their friends and be liked, instead of being respected. It was easier to go along and avoid confrontation than provide the proper discipline. Many parents tended to coddle and overindulge their offspring producing undisciplined spoiled brats. Of the hundreds of parents we interviewed, a majority of them failed to set firm rules and never taught their children to respect and obey. The parents finally agreed and told their son that we were in charge. Their acquiescence also made us the bad guys and conveniently removed them from the picture. Dago Don went to work with a pair of scissors, and the boy's tail was no more. I admonished him to have his stud and nose ring removed before he showed up on Saturday, or he would be dropped.

To go one step further, I told the boy to look up the term "aborigine" and to write me an essay on why he wanted to identify himself with a Neanderthal primitive culture. The need for a sense of identity among many of these kids was so strong that even self degradation wasn't off the table.

Since many of our philandering flock were referred because they were tardy and truant, we made house calls and school visits regularly. Our friendly visits also led to a drop in vehicle and residential burglaries during day time hours committed by boys who were supposed to be in school. We covered these kids' necks like a bottle cap, and often knew more about their activities than their mothers, and, sadly, their fathers. When we caught them dirty or "toking up" we would not bust them, but rather gave them extra hours. They had to learn, just like in real life, there are consequences to their actions. We were almost like a second shadow to the most hardcore of these kids. Similar to Batman and Robin, we would show up anywhere and everywhere. In some cases we were also like guardian angels when they got jammed up. The bottom line was that we wanted them to understand that we were there for them before it was too late!

This brings me to the story of the devil and Danny Dominguez. I made a house call at the parents' request of a kid dubbed "defiant" Danny. Danny was clicked-up – he was a gang member – and his parents feared that the hammer was about to fall; only it wasn't a ball peen. Glock would be more like it. I tore into him in the living room and his parents made a quick exit. Danny's eyes went from defiant to deadly. His face filled with hate and harm. Now he was Lucifer's nowhere man. The eyes that met mine were no longer Danny's.

If this were a play, it would be called "Danny Dominguez and the Holy Face." I was in over my head, and I knew it. Backup was needed, but men in blue wouldn't do. The enemy was not of this world. In desperation I made a mad grab for a picture of Jesus which stood watch on the mantle place. In a scene blown right out of "The Exorcist," I shoved the holy face of Jesus right up to Danny's deadly eyes. The Prince of Peace collided head on with the Prince of Darkness.

"Heaven or hell Danny, which one is it going to be?" I angrily shouted.

An eerie foreboding silence answered me. Would it be deity or devil that scored the knock out punch? Angry and fearful of the holy face, the devil in Danny departed. The boy stood up and beckoned me to his room where he instructed me to open a dresser drawer. I did so, and removed a gun that had its' serial numbers shaved off. A hit had been placed on a rival gang member and Danny was to deliver the bullet that would bite.

We immediately rushed Danny out of town to safety. A lucky lad got to live another day, and for Danny, a life was found just as it was about to be lost. This line

PHOTOGRAPHS

GRANDPARENTS

SHOOTS AT BANDITS AND THEY KILL HIM

Peddler Fires as He Comes Upon Hold-Up Men Who Had Just Robbed Another.

FEARED BLACK HAND BAND

Victim Had Received Threats and Thought Trio Had Come for Him, Police Say.

In the belief he was confronting black handers, Salvatore Dippaolo, 35 years old, a peddler, of 411 East Sixtieth Street, yesterday opened fire on three men who had just bound and gagged another peddler in a stable at 412 East Fifty-ninth Street. He was shot dead.

A few minutes before, the three men had entered the stable as James Giulio, a vegetable peddler, of 321 East Sixtieth Street, was preparing to take out his horse and wagon. With pistols at his head, Giulio gave the robbers $60, pleading for his life.

He was bound and gagged and thrown against the wall of a stall. As his assailants were asking him when the other peddlers would arrive, Dippaolo came in. Two months ago Dippaolo had received a black-hand letter in which money had been demanded and which contained a threat against the lives of his wife and four children.

Because of this Dippaolo had bought a pistol, though he did not obtain a permit. The police believe that Dippaolo feared the black handers had come for him and therefore drew his weapon and fired one shot, which went wild. The three hold-up men immediately fired one shot each at Dippaolo. One hit him above the heart and a second in his left arm.

The murderers fled to the street and shouted to a passing taxicab, but the driver had heard the shots and sped away. Later the police found him and he was taken to Police Headquarters to examine Rogues Gallery photographs. The robbery escaped into Avenue A.

NEW YORK TIMES - DECEMBER 2, 1923

FATHER

SON

UNDERCOVER AS FRANKIE APOLLO (1979)

HOLLYWOOD PATROL

PREPPED FOR LA RIOTS

"GANGBUSTERS"

WITH PARTNER TOM BROOKS (1976)

WITH GOVERNOR PETE WILSON AND ROBERT ROBLES

WITH FORMER GOVERNORS PETE WILSON
AND ARNOLD SCHWARZENEGGER

WITH ABC'S LYNN SHER OF "20/20"

ON THE SET OF "JAKE AND THE FATMAN"

WITH YARA AND DENNIS FRANZ OF "NYPD BLUE"

EAST LA PAINT-OUT

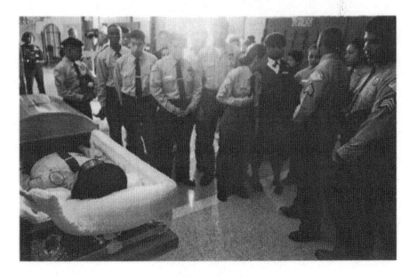

ABEL'S FUNERAL

YARA WITH HER EAST LA GIRLS

WITH YARA AND JUVENILE IMPACT PROGRAM KIDS

WITH LOCO LOPEZ

WITH MANNY MARTINEZ

"FATHER STEVE"
REV. JOSEPH MUDD, C.P. (1948-1990)

YARA AND FRANK DiPAOLA WITH THE Z-28 CAMARO

comes to mind: "Son, behold the time and fly from evil." *(Ecclesiastes 10:23)*

DEADLY ART
Graffiti is the expression of a ghetto which is near to the plague,
for civilization is now inimical to the ghetto.
— NORMAN MAILER

To most of us, it just looks like lousy urban scrawl. Sadly the menacing messages on the walls of buildings, buses, freeways, and railroad cars are often a billboard of criminal activity. It is the language of the street, an urban tattoo; a wrong-way search for identity. Romantic elusive scribbling of "Dick loves Jane" and the innocent "Kilroy was here" of the 1940's were benign and harmless. Today's messages are framed in pathology of the tough and deadly.

I am going to give you a basic 101 class of graffiti as Don and I learned it firsthand from the taggers and gangsters themselves. Graffiti consists of two main types: tagger graffiti and gang graffiti. The intended purposes of both are at opposite ends of the spectrum. Rome was conquered by Huns and Vandals from without. Our Huns and Vandals are bred from within, which makes the situation even more disconcerting and dangerous. The term 'vandalism' is taken directly from the sacking of ancient Rome by the Vandals. The Vandals were a Germanic barbarian tribe that invaded Rome in 270 A.D. and again in 455 A.D., leaving much of the city in ruins.

Modern day Huns and Vandals, taggers and gangsters, also lay waste to our cities and towns armed with the menacing spray can as their weapon of destruction. They are also often a catalyst to violent confrontations. Gangs and their members are no different from the tribal warlords of days of old. History repeats itself because we don't get any smarter.

Our urban anthropology 101 course will provide an insight into this destructive culture. I used the term 'culture' loosely. We had to understand the language of the street which defined their criminal activity.

The term "tag" or "tagger" means tough artist group. Tagger graffiti is put up for the purpose of fame. The more places "it's up," the more fame and respect the tagger reaps. Taggers either work in crews or perform solo. From a historical perspective, it is believed that the first tagger was a young kid from New York named "Taki." In 1973 he was a messenger and began spray painting "Taki 183" (the 183 was his house number) throughout the boroughs of New York. Taki especially liked buses, billboards, and trains as his canvas. A writer for the New York Times did a better piece of police work than the police did in tracking him down, and wrote an expose on him. The article gave Taki the fame he craved, and wrongly inspired kids all over New York to also become tagging folk heroes. The tagging stage was now set. Thanks to the hip-hop "no-culture" culture on TV and videos, tagging and its stupid destructive lifestyle spread to Los Angeles and to other American cities.

I was featured on a series on graffiti on ABC's 20/20 where I was interviewed extensively by anchor Lynn Sher over a four-day filming. Much of the information that follows is similar to that which aired on the TV segment.

Tagger motivation is a quest for fame and identity; a need to be recognized. I have interviewed hundreds of taggers who are so addicted to spraying their stuff that many actually suck on the spray can tips, or "nipples," as they are called. Many taggers often have a fresh nipple in their mouth at all times in case the one they are using jams. The tips can be modified to affect the size of the area tagged. Taggers start with a stock tip and use fingertip measurements categorized as the number 2, 3, or 4 fingertips. A 4-inch fingertip emits a wider spray than a 2-inch fingertip. Serious taggers will have flared tips and fat caps, or "professional tips" in their arsenal of destruction.

Most taggers consider themselves to be artists and selfishly believe that their "pieces" are so good that they should be able to put them up wherever they so desire. I once debated a former tagger who called himself a graffiti artist on a TV show called "Life and Times." His view was that the city should provide taggers wall space so they could express themselves and not face prosecution. This stupid entitlement mentality is ludicrous, I countered.

"Getting up" where it is illegal and there's risk factor involved, like on bridges, provides the taggers with a rush or high. Taggers also go to great lengths to be "up," such as dangling from a rope to tag a freeway sign, or an inaccessible billboard, or building. The more dangerous the location to be tagged, the greater the rush and the accompanying fame. Many taggers have died in this crazy quest to find their misplaced identity-slash-manhood.

Taggers who put up pieces are sometimes quite talented, versus the ones who just scrawl their tag name. Unlike most bad guys, taggers want to be known, so tracking them down is usually easier than other criminals. Don and I threw ourselves headfirst into the thick of the universe of graffiti and gangs. When we were dope cops, we would immerse ourselves into back issues of High Times, the monthly magazine which is a bible of dope lore. I would also hang out at head shops and soak up the venomous vocabulary of dope fiends. "Cronic," "bud," "bindles," and "bongs" became part of my vocabulary.

The graffiti world was no different, so we jumped in. Every tagger and gangster we arrested was debriefed. They taught us different styles of writing and the slang terms they used. We eventually developed a tagger file of over five hundred tagging names. It was easy to make snitches out of many of the taggers who fell prey to the two Dagos, and many crimes were solved. We developed the most extensive tagger file that LAPD ever possessed. One infamous tagging crew whose tag was "FBI" drew the ire of, you guessed it, the L.A. Field Office of the real FBI. The reality was that the tag, which showed up on freeways all over the city, stood for "freeway busters insane."

Don and I got so adept at deciphering these highway hieroglyphics that often we could read a tag and almost immediately recognize its author. We made the big time when we were contacted by a reporter for World News Tonight with Peter Jennings. This was the first national news show that featured us. Prior investigations had led us to bust a tagger named "Blank" who had recently completed his hours in our program. The ABC News crew had "tagged" along (oops, no pun intended) with our juvenile chain gang to buff (paint out) a neighborhood that had been bombed. One of the tags that defaced the area was "Knalb." We immediately recognized the writing as belonging to "Blank." He spelled his name backwards to throw us off his track. The moniker belonged to a freckled-faced scarecrow of a kid named Bengy.

When our black-'n-white pulled up to Bengy's pad he greeted us with a not so confident, "Uh, what's up?"

"You are, Bengy baby, all over the hood. Put your hands behind your back, and you're under arrest again," I advised.

Blank went Blank, and let go with a surprised, "How did ya know it was me?" Bengy agreed to do 200 hours this time. One hundred hours for the graffiti and another hundred for the double dago double cross.

At this juncture it's time to introduce our urban anthropology dictionary of graffiti terminology. Learn them well: There is a quiz at the end of this chapter.

"ALL CITY"	TAGGER WHOSE MONIKER IS IN MANY DIFFERENT NEIGHBORHOODS.
"BATTLE"	RIVALRY BETWEEN TAGGING CREWS TO SEE WHO CAN PUT UP MORE TAGS IN AN ALLOTTED AMOUNT OF TIME.
"DRIVER SIDE"	WRITING GRAFFITI ON THE TRAFFIC SIDE OF A BUS.
"FADE"	BLENDING COLORS.
"REACHING THE HEAVENS"	TAGS PUT UP ON HIGH PLACES.
C WITH A CIRCLE	COPYRIGHTED TAG.
"HIT"	TO TAG A SURFACE.
"MOB"	MANY TAGGERS HITTING A NEIGHBORHOOD.
"MUSHROOM"	INNOCENT PERSON WHO POPS UP DURING A TAG AND GETS IN THE WAY.

| "KILL" | EXCESSIVE TAGGING OF A LOCATION. |
| "SLASH" | CROSSING OUT ANOTHER TAGGERS NAME. |

There's more of this Neanderthal stupidity, but I think you get the idea. This misplaced and baseless quest for fame has also led to many taggers being killed, either by rival taggers, or gangsters who claim that section of the "hood." Many tagging crews, who once just wanted notoriety, became gangs by removing the name "kings" from their crew name and substituting the word "killers." Some street gangs, to increase their membership, held an open enrollment and incorporated entire tagging crews into their gang. The crazier or the more violent a tagger or gang member becomes, the more respect or fame he gets.

This leads us to the next phase of graffiti and its violent perpetuator, the gangster. Gang graffiti is bold and is meant to intimidate. Tagging is meant to be stylistic using a "bubble" or "burner" style. Gang graffiti will be bold and sometimes use the old English or block letter style.

California penal code section 186.22 defines a gang as the following: an ongoing group or association involving three or more subjects, informal or formal, in order to perpetuate criminal activity. The following statistics will put the enormity of the gang problem in perspective. The city of Los Angeles has approximately 39,000 gang members in 465 gangs. According to Cal-Gang, a statewide data base, there are over 350,000 gang members in the state of California. L.A. County has 85,000 gang members in over 1,000 different gangs. The U.S. as a whole boasts 800,000 gang members in over 30,000 different gangs. According to the National Threat Assessment of 2011, gangs are responsible for an average of 48% of violent crime in most jurisdictions and up to 90% in several others. More than half of law enforcement agencies reporting to the National Gang Intelligence Center report an increase in gang activity in their jurisdictions over the past two years.

Gang graffiti, more so than the taggers' scrawl, tend to be billboards of criminal activity. For example, the California penal code for murder, which is 187, may be accompanied by an X through a rival gang's name. This would indicate that a murder has taken place, or is about to occur of that gang by a rival gang. Most gang members have a placaso or placa (a nickname or gang moniker) which is usually associated with a physical or other characteristic of the individual gangster. For example: if the gang member is balding, or has a shaved head, he may be called pelon (Spanish for bald headed) or wino if he likes his booze.

Loco, or crazy in Spanish, is another common placa. In the gang dictionary mi vida loca or my crazy life is a common Hispanic gang term. In gang non-culture, the crazier a gangster is the more esteem and respect may be earned from his compadres.

Juero or white is often a moniker for a light skinned Hispanic. Snoopy, after the carton character, is also commonly used. A list of these monikers or placasos, alongside a gang graffiti piece, would usually indicate the gang member's presence when the piece was put up. This is termed a "roll call," and the name appearing on top is the one who did the writing. If a shooting is committed in the vicinity of a rival gang member, the "roll call" is a good place for the investigation of the shooter's identity to begin. We had moniker and graffiti files on virtually every gang in Northeast along with the street "creds" to keep the info pipeline wide open.

We earned our respect on the street by treating the taggers and gang members with respect. We were tough but fair. Being a bully or badge heavy was never our m.o., and should not be in a good street policemen's playbook. Gangsters only respect those who they love or fear. They often equate respect with fear, not good attributes. The sad thing is that many of these kids never had the time to be kids. Now they are trying to act like men and don't know how.

Since gangsters don't normally have a love thing for cops, fear and fair is the basis for their respect. Gangsters are identified more by who they hate than by who they are. Too often you can't kill the hate; it hangs on you like a dose of bad breath.

Adventures in graffiti, like police work itself, went from the ridiculous to the sublime. How's this for ridiculous: the paint we used was usually donated, so the colors varied. We tried to mix and match, but Dunn Edwards we were not. On one smog-filled Saturday, we came upon a neighborhood that had recently been heavily bombed. Even the trees had graffiti on them. Along with the objects tagged were several city vehicles and a construction trailer.

They were originally painted City of Los Angeles yellow, but were now tagged to the max. The only color we had was green, so guess what? The kids got a little too happy with the hand rollers, and the vehicles got a new make over in green.

L.A. was a circus, and we were the ringmasters...or even maybe the clowns. Our fun-filled graffiti rehab adventure tour often caused humorous humdingers. The two Dagos often broke out in a burst of raucous, perverse laughter. On another occasion, our dead-end devils dispatched themselves to buff out a dismal duplex in go-bright green. With all the commotion, several of the tenants were beckoned to their windows to observe the crew's calamity. In Spanish a male voice yelled, "Que pasa?" In English a female voice responded, "It's the police. They are painting the building green." After the laughter we just shook our heads at the complacency and normalcy of the abnormal and absurd.

Welcome to my world!

FATHER STEVE, THE PASSIONATE PASSIONIST

Charity begins at home, and justice begins next door.
— CHARLES DICKENS

Yara and I usually went to Mass on Sundays, but that was about the extent of our religious activities. Although we were strong believers and were married in the church, "holy rollers" we were not.

We attended Mass at our parish, the beautiful, Romanesque St. Andrew's Catholic Church, in Pasadena. It had elegant marble columns and a hallowed travertine altar. One day an announcement from the pulpit caught my attention. The Passionist Retreat House in nearby Sierra Madre was inviting the men of the parish to attend a spiritual retreat. Having never been on a retreat, but fully aware that my wanting soul needed a spiritual tune-up, I went for it.

The official name of the retreat house is Mater Delarosa (Mother of Sorrows) Passionist Monastery. The monastery dates from 1924 and is nestled neatly in the San Gabriel Mountains at an elevation of 1200 feet. Sweeping views reach to the horizon from downtown L.A. in the southwest then eastward to the outer reaches of the San Gabriel Valley. Somebody should post a sign with the following warning: views are dependent on daily dirty air smog alerts. The view could be fifty miles or fifty feet.

In the early days the monastery was called Mt. Olivette, and one could definitely be stirred to an acute sense of the Divine and even heaven itself. The 1200 foot elevation didn't hurt the ambiance either. Neatly tucked in behind the holy house of God are the majestic San Gabriel Mountains ascending to the heavens above in a pastoral reach; a ladder without steps.

I arrived on a Friday night for a weekend sojourn along with some seventy-five other hungry male souls looking for a diet of spirituality. The retreat master and pastoral prince of this holy house on the hill was a super clean-cut guy with close cropped hair and strikingly-happy blue eyes.

His name was Father Steve, and his bold smile was the gateway to a hearty laugh and a great gregarious personality. The guy immediately held steam with me. He was a chap you could like without working at it. Father Steve was different. No fiery hell and damnation sermons, but no warm and fuzziness either. He was plain old straight talk from a loving heart and tremendous intellect. Father Steve emphasized that this was a silent retreat. The outside world stresses self gratification and self indulgence. In here, we stress self mortification and contemplation in an effort to bring us closer to God.

If we were to do any talking at all it would be to God. "Silence, respectful silence" signs adorned the walls along with numerous Biblical quotes. The quote on the wall above my bed said it all, "He who believes in Me though he dies will live forever." Another quote from Isaiah, "The Lord God makes death banish and life eternal." I thought to myself that these were uplifting thoughts which take the finality out of dying for the believer.

Father Steve called the retreat a faith tune-up. One of the themes of the retreat was that the word Catholic means universal. We are an inclusive faith reaching out to everyone. Not a faith of exclusivity. We are not just about worshipping and praying. While that is very important, our faith must also be accompanied by good works and reaching out to others. If you want the "E-ticket" to heaven you're going to have to hit the streets.

The two main points emphasized in this retreat, which are the genesis of the Catholic faith, are "Love your neighbor as yourself" and "God so loved the world that He gave his only Son so that everyone who believed in Him might not perish, but have eternal life." The paradox of Christianity is that in death we find life. That's the bottom line, Father Steve emphasized with a sincere smile. "So why not get out the pen and sign on the dotted line?"

The seminar was followed by quiet time so we could stroll the beautiful gardens and reflect on the messages. I welcomed the silence routine, too. In my work world full of noise, it was a welcomed respite, although it did take some getting used to. Meditative muteness wasn't one of my strongest points, but solace and serenity from the outside world encased the place like a wool comforter from Granny's attic. There was such a spirit of holiness about the monastery that the devil himself couldn't creep in.

Another retreat theme centered on the ever-present Biblical term "Emmanuel," which means, "God is with us." This gives rise to the scriptural passage, "And the word was made flesh." Even though I had heard this often I never really understood what it meant. Father Steve explained that it referred to God assuming our human form through Jesus, who is both God and man. To take it a step further, the image of God is in all of us, from the lowliest beggar to the most holy of people.

I rolled my eyes on that one and let go with a "Yeah, right" under my breath. This was really a stretch for a street cop dealing daily with the hideous and the heinous. If he said the image of the devil was in each and every one of us I would have bought it with an easy swallow. Some private time with Father Steve was needed for a further revelation. My one-eyed skepticism jumped right out at him. He was good natured about it, though.

"Faith can shape the way people behave and counter evil," he explained. "Faith fills life with meaning and purpose, and we are all called to be part of the human drama by reflecting the face of Christ in all those that we meet." It occurred to me that He was inside of me but I was outside of myself.

Then, in his infinite wisdom, he threw out a quote from C. S. Lewis: "There are no ordinary people. You never met a mere mortal." He finished with that confident smile of his, and I think I got it. I needed to ratchet up my faith and start looking at humanity from a different perspective. It wouldn't be easy, but I'd certainly give it a try. The retreat concluded with Father Steve bellowing, "Isn't Jesus great? He takes the sting out of dying."

I always figured a good shot of Jack Daniels did that, but then again, at the end of the run, might be no time for J.D. If you bought what the preacher man was selling, J.C. might just be the ticket.

Father Steve was like no other priest I have ever met, and we immediately hit it off. We became good friends. When he was off duty he told me to knock off the "Father" stuff and just go with Steve. He enjoyed a drink as much as the next guy and would join Yara and me for an occasional happy hour. He always had a seat at our dinner table with his name on it.

* * * * *

Police work creates a mine field of manure to maneuver through. After all the years of down and dirty, I was dragging on the people parade. The venomous vibes from the hell-bent homies and two-bit gangster wannabes were like a deluge of diarrhea.

Even after the retreat a nagging thought persisted: "Is man basically good or evil?" I confessed to Steve – and not in the box but over a couple of pops – that I still had lingering thoughts about this good and evil thing.

"In the end it's up to us. When we get bogged down with life we can hand the ball to God and He will run with it. Kind of like an insurance policy, but you got to buy the policy," he explained.

His answer shined some skylight into the dark tunnel I was edging my way out of, but I needed a spotlight, not a flashlight. The light would eventually come, but I wasn't there yet.

When it comes to Mexican grazing spots and magnificent margaritas, the Fiesta Grande on Colorado Boulevard, was the best in the West. That's right, the same boulevard where the "Little Old Lady from Pasadena" once cruised. Father Steve and I parked ourselves there after hours and on weekends when he wasn't manning the monastery. In between salted lime-topped margaritas, the good and evil conundrum surfaced again.

"Look," Father Steve offered up with his usual smile and knowing eyes, "Man has had a fallen nature since Adam and his girlfriend got in bed with the serpent. You know the rest. Obviously in your line of work you're familiar with the idea that 'there is a little larceny in everybody,' right?"

I nodded in agreement. "I would be in the unemployment line if that weren't the case."

"Okay," he continued in between munching on salsa-soaked chips, "We all have the propensity for evil and this thing we call free will either gives in to temptation, or it doesn't. The devil from the deep blue sea sneaks in when you're not looking, wets the pallet with a little luscious temptation, and bingo, you're slammed! Over-simplified perhaps, but that's it in a New York nutshell."

"I think I'm getting it, God didn't want to create a bunch of slaves. He wanted us to choose the right thing out of love for Him, not because we are robots."

"You got it," Steve said, as the bottom of the long-stemmed margarita holder pushed closer to that boyish grin. "Enough of this holy shop stuff: let's order – I'm hungry."

That's how it went with Father Steve. He would lead you to the pond but you had to jump in on your own. His genuine smile was as infectious as his personality. When you had a God question, he had a God answer in ten seconds or less. We would get together for a few pops at least once a week with just enough holy banter to tweak the intellect and stir the soul.

Father Steve and I had many bartenders in town that were very dependent on us. One of our favorites was named Mike Magillicutty, affectionately nicknamed "Malarkey Mike" at Monahan's. He was a robust, jolly soul who resembled a beer keg on legs. Mike got a real kick out of our weekly cop and clergy routine, and enjoyed soaking up a little true crime and spirituality, as Father Steve and I soaked up the suds. Blarney and beer go together like burgers and beer, and Monahan's was the perfect neighborhood nest – a tawny tavern that the locals called home and was once dubbed Pasadena's finest watering hole. The name fit because it had more lagers on tap than you could down in a day. Pithy quotes by the not-so-famous adorned the faded mahogany walls, giving the patrons something to think about between swigs. One quote that always caught my eye went something like this: "I live my life, I love my life, and my critics be damned." Arrogant perhaps, but I liked it. It would make a good epitaph.

"The ancient monks brewed beer in ancient monasteries," Malarkey Mike offered up, as I was downing my second I.P.A. (India Pale Ale).

He offered up another history lesson, "Ya know how that brew you're drinking got its name?"

"No idea Mike, but it's got just the right bite," I answered.

"When the Brits were in India, their troops had a deep longing for their home brew, so the pubs back home shipped it all the way to India to keep 'em happy. By time it got there, it turned pale," he said.

"Thanks, Michael me boy. It tastes better now that I know I'm drinking a piece of history."

Father Steve was on his third, so I was playing catch up.

"Tap room theology ain't only good for the whistle-wettin' but it don't hurt the soul either. You guys ought to come around more often. This religious stuff is catchy. I might slip from the 'holly and lily crowd' and get church goin' regular-like," Mike told us in his Irish brogue.

"Yeah, and we'd become a couple of drunks on a sea of booze. You know what would happen then, Mike?" I asked jokingly.

"No, so why don't you tell me so I won't have to keep guessing?" Mike asked.

"The boat would sink."

The blarney and beer were flowing pretty good, there was even some holy smoke floating up from our marvelous Maduros.

The holy smoke ushered in some holy and not so light banter.

"How's the kid program down at the station going?" Father Steve asked between puffs.

"Great. We are getting a pound of flesh out of them. They play, they pay. Push-up's and paint."

Malarkey Mike felt compelled to throw in his two cents. "Yeah, these kids get away with murder today: no discipline, no consequences, and no respect."

Father Steve put what was left of the Maduro to rest in the black ceramic ashtray with the Monahan's logo which read, "Where friends meet for great steaks and chops." He looked me directly in the eye and frowned. "Why don't you reach out to these kids? Father figures and role models are in short supply; maybe you could even save a few souls! Frank, if you are really able to step out of yourself, a guy like you could probably save a small chunk of humanity. Just being there for them with a little mentoring thrown in would probably go a long way. It might just be the catalyst to pull them out of the hole. Redemption if you will."

"Steve, I'm all for helping kids but I'm a cop. Saving souls is your business."

He laughed. "Saving souls is everybody's business. Remember the retreat and the universal theme? Men's souls need to be fed as well as their bodies. That's what it means to help the poor in spirit. Many of these kids may not need food or clothes, but they are sure as hell wanting spiritually."

When he mentioned saving mankind it reminded me of that scene in Charles Dickens's "A Christmas Carol," where Scrooge blurts out to the two gentlemen asking for a donation to help wayward boys, "Are there no prisons? Are there no work houses?" To which one of the gentlemen responds, "Saving mankind is everybody's business."

I guess that I just had been scrooged. Father Steve was on a roll. "I don't want to get too heavy with the cultural collapse routine, but there is a major crisis of humanity today. Call it poor parenting or no parenting and a decadent deluge of media madness. All this is being absorbed by young mushy minds with no frame of reference to the morality of the way things used to be. Hell, you ought to hear the things these kids tell me in the confessional. Rich or poor, most of them are behind the eight ball right out of the shoot. They think loving one another means taking the 'A' train to a flesh feast."

"Yeah, I know, Steve. When I was a kid I thought a head job meant getting the valves re-worked on Pop's old Buick. I thought I got lucky when I was sixteen if I copped a back seat cheap feel at the Valley Stream Drive-in."

Father Steve went on, "Today that's child's play. They are copping at six, oral at eight and full bore at twelve. I told a ninth grader that her body was sacred and a temple of God. She answered with a bewildered, 'Huh?' These kids are hurting so much inside. They are morally bankrupt, but it's out of not knowing. Change starts with the heart, not necessarily with the mind. There is so little love in their lives. How are they going to know how to give love if they don't receive it? Love means being vulnerable, and the homies you deal with can't get that emotional. It's a sign of weakness."

I was just cruising for some light bar room chatter, but this, "he ain't heavy he's my brother routine" was starting to load the scale.

Father Steve rarely quoted scripture, but this time he couldn't help himself. "In John's gospel, Jesus said to his disciples: 'Love one another as I have loved you.' And in that same passage (*John 15:12-17*) 'It was not you who chose me but I who chose you. This I command you, love one another.' Don't you get it? Your downward career spiral brought you to this place. It's a combination of dramatic irony and a Divine dramatic dragnet."

Now I did the bewildered, "Huh, what does Jack Webb have to do with this?"

"You wanted nothing to do with kids, right?"

"Right."

"Well sometimes God chooses the most unlikely people to do His bidding and maybe, just maybe, He chose you. The kingdom of heaven is like a net thrown into the sea. The early fishermen would drag their nets to the shore and that's where the term dragnet came from. Your ace detective, Sgt. Joe Friday, was derived from the sea story. The good fish were kept and the bad ones discarded. Maybe it was no accident that you ran into your old friend Captain Carl and he dragged you off to Northeast."

"I'm picking up a little heaven and hell thing, Steve. Am I on the right track?"

"You are, my friend. You were plucked from the LAPD big blue sea before you drowned, for the specific purpose of reaching out to others. Don't forget that when Jesus started His earthly ministry He sent His followers to be fishers of men."

"Another sea analogy," I chuckled. "It doesn't matter if you're a priest, a cop, or Mike the bartender."

"How'd I get into this?" Mike laughed.

Theology on tap; I was tapped out, but I got it.

"Another round, Mike," I ordered.

"Maybe God is giving you an invitation and a challenge. In turn you can provide an invitation and challenge to those kids you're dealing with. See if they bite," Father Steve said. Words poured from his lips as easily as a bartender's beer tap.

"What's the difference between a thermometer and a thermostat?" Steve asked with that self-assured all knowing smile that he was famous for.

"A thermostat changes the temperature. A thermometer measures it." I responded matter-of-factly. "What's that got to do with anything?"

He was right back at me, "You have a hell of an opportunity to change these kids from hate to love. Maybe you are God's mouthpiece for the good news. Like the thermostat you can change these kids. So go for it, man."

This was getting way too heavy for even Malarkey Mike, so when he brought over the next foam topped ale he threw in a shot of "Gentlemen Jack."

"You're going to need this boilermaker before you're through," Mike said.

"Look guys, Romans 13 cuts to the chase. All the commandments are basically summed up in this one: 'You shall love your neighbor as yourself. Love does no evil to the neighbor,'" Father Steve quoted.

"Amen and hallelujah!" Mike exclaimed with a chuckle.

Father Steve also chuckled and turned to me with his pair of penetrating eyes and said, "I don't commit a lot of Ezekiel to memory, but I think he speaks to the both of us with this one, 'Oh wicked one, you shall surely die if you don't speak out to dissuade the wicked one from his way, the wicked one shall die from his guilt but I will hold you responsible for his death.'" (*Ezekiel 33:7-9*)

I didn't know if I was numb from the boilermakers or the Bible.

"Use your badge as a pulpit, you silver tongued devil," Father Steve continued as he finished his last beer. "You got the dynamite, so you may as well light the fuse."

This liquor-loaded repartee became the cornerstone of my future. Locked into place when my barroom buddy and monastic mentor was taken by a malicious malignancy which eventually overcame his body. But it could never penetrate his soul. On our last visit together he was as upbeat and gregarious as usual.

I was not. "Why you Steve, why did God...?"

He quickly cut me off, "It's got nothing to do with God. It's the human condition. Besides, with the little time I have left I can really concentrate on what God wants me to do with no distractions. It has been said that the greatest gift tragedy brings us is that it forces you to consider the things you took for granted. The important thing to remember is that if we unite our sufferings with Christ we contribute to the salvation of others. Kind of taking away the pain of people we don't even know. Let me put it in another way. Sickness and suffering conforms us in a way to Christ crucified. As Saint Therese of the Child Jesus (the Little Flower) so eloquently put it, 'Suffering helps detach us from the material things of this earth, and makes us look higher than this world. Besides, life and pain in this world are a short run, and tomorrow is forever, and we shall be at rest.' Death and suffering seen through the right lens is okay. Love life but embrace death."

It was then that this good man's divinity deeply touched my humanity. A few short weeks later I got a Christmas card from him. That Christmas of long ago is still vivid in my memory. It was bittersweet because he wasn't with us to share Christmas dinner. In his Christmas card he explained how God has touched him in a special way through his illness and that he will continue to pray for Yara and me. Most people in his condition would ask others to pray for them, but instead he was praying for us. Words of St. Francis of Assisi came to mind: "Sister death is the open door to life – eternal life." He was a priest to the end. He even added a P.S.: "Don't forget what you are going to do with the gifts God gave you."

My good friend passed away shortly thereafter.

Malarkey Mike still kept busy, however, because even though Father Steve's bar stool stood empty, I did the drinking for both of us. The ghost of gregarious laughter, that soul of wit, was right there besides me.

GOD, GANGS, AND LOCO LOPEZ

It costs so little to teach a child to love, and so much to teach him to hate.
— FATHER FLANAGAN

The short swarthy Mexican kid from the barrio ran hard and fast. In the ghetto, you get plenty of practice; you are always in training. The huda (slang term for police) and hood rats, or rival homies, are always on your tail trying to make you or break you. In the hood, his placaso was Loco Mr. Silent. No wino or pee-wee or even just plain loco, of which there were several. He had class, and the Mr. Silent gave him that.

The spray-painted graffiti was still fresh Mr. Silent p/v (abbreviation por vida which means for life) when Officer Miguel "Macho" Moreno spotted his prey and gave chase. Captain Carl had assigned "Macho," who usually worked the school car, to round up the usual graffiti suspects for club impact. The Captain wanted to make an impact, no pun intended, on Northeast's graffiti problem and let the homies know that the cops meant business.

Officer "Macho" Moreno never met a mirror he didn't like. When he wasn't so self-indulged or power-lifting in the weight room, he was trolling for made-up mujeres (women) or homies that needed to get arrested. The neighborhood cholitas (tough women) were ferocious at flirting with any gringo or Mexican cop that was svelte, handsome, and under 35. The fact that "Macho's" bulging biceps barely forced their way into the short sleeves of an LAPD blue suit didn't hurt. "Macho" caught up with Loco at Avenue 43 and Figueroa. There was a tumultuous tackle, and both became one with the pavement. "Macho" angrily clamped the cuffs on Loco's reluctant wrists and escorted him back to his black-'n-white taxi cab for a free one-way ride.

Score one for "Macho" and zero for Loco. As the black-'n-white eased up to the rear door of the station to spill out its gangster humanity, Don and I activated the P.A. on our black-'n-white. We let go with a solo version of "Macho Macho Man." Loco and "Macho" were not happy campers, and their brief time together was definitely no love-fest. Loco, because he would be deprived of another day or more of spray painting, dope-dealing, or other insidious activities. Loco missed the humor from our Village People routine as he tumbled defiantly from the black-'n-white with a bruised knee and ego to match. "Macho" wasn't too happy about his uniform, which now needed a trip to the cleaners for a clean and press job.

"Los pinchi placas" (the fucking cops) Loco muttered under his breath. No, definitely not a love-fest between these two. Loco straightened himself up and held his head high, trying to catch any last bit of passing pride that he still had left.

"This sucker ran from me, felony stupid and he got the scars to prove it," "Macho" triumphantly stated.

"I guess you didn't know you were dealing with a gorilla, huh, kid? You fought the law, and the law won," I said with a grin. Loco still wasn't laughing. As I said, his moniker is Mr. Silent, which distinguished him from the other Locos in his hood.

"I'll put him in the holding cell and write it up," "Macho" Moreno offered.

The dark and dingy holding cell which Loco would call home for the next hour or two rivaled his mood. Loco and several other usual gang-banger suspects, rounded up in a Highland Park street cleaning exercise, were pissed-off. Really pissed-off! I unlocked the cell door and motioned to Loco to come out. He turned to his "cellies" and angrily let out the following:

"What's this fool want?" as he motioned towards me. Obviously we did not begin this relationship on terms of endearment. Socrates once said that, "Wisdom begins in the recognition of how little we know." I always begin any interrogation or interview by building a rapport, and than getting the perps to talk about themselves as much as possible.

"Who do you kick it with?" I asked matter-of-factly about who his associates were, even though I already knew.

His snub-nose frame was clothed in dickies colored in blue and a belt buckle which proudly displayed the letter of his gang on a silver metal background. A moco rag was draped over his belt. With his accompanying attitude he could have been a poster boy for gangster magazine.

"I'm solo. I don't kick it with nobody," he snapped back at me.

Loco's real name was Louie Lopez, and he sported the three-dot tattoo in triangular fashion on his hand, between the thumb and forefinger representing mi vida loca or my crazy life.

He was ganged up all right, and belonged to one of the oldest gangs in East L.A. Loco was definitely living up to his name. I didn't have to tell him, "You have the right to remain silent." He knew the drill. I proceeded to question him.

"How old are you Louie?"

"Seventeen, so you can't send me to county. Juvy ain't nothin' I can hang, so do what you gotta do bro!"

Loco, like most gangsters, was defiant, especially with cops. Everybody in this life wants to be special. If you aren't special because of brains or a certain talent, its because you're a tough guy. Defiance and toughness were pounded into Loco like carpenter's nails on an A-frame. The more Loco hated, the better his street rep. When the police confront this defiance with defiance of their own, a mutual hate society is formed and little is accomplished. When I confronted Loco, my eyes shouted tough but genuine. The key with gangsters is not to push the hate hot button but to understand why they hate. Diagnosing is just as important as it is when fixing a car. If you know why it's broken, hopefully you can get to the what.

"What I got to do Louie is save your ass, and I ain't your bro, so the next time it's 'officer.' Got it?"

"Why you care about me?" Louie replied with a haughty hint of self-pity.

I answered him in homie talk that I was becoming all too familiar with and which he could relate to. "You ain't got the heart of a killer. Your eyes are telling me more than your mouth."

Louie was a guy that I wanted to like, even if I had to work at it. I knew I could get to him, but it would be a long hard drive. It was all about respect, which is why he probably joined a gang in the first place. Respect comes from love or fear. He had to fear me before he could love me.

"Louie, I'll tell you what. We got a program here that I started called Impact to help kids like you. We buff out graffiti and try to keep you guys from ending up in the joint or in a box." I stuck out my hand and offered up, "If you're in for 100 hours with the cops, I'll forget about the arrest report that Officer Moreno is writing up."

"What I gotta do?" He asked with a faint hint of sincerity.

"Complete the program. You played, you pay. Just like gang-banging...with a big difference." I replied.

"What's that?" he asked.

"We want to save you, not bury you." I responded with my truth wide open.

Loco finally unclenched his intestines and gave up the Mr. Silent routine.

"Yeah, sign me up. But I still don't trust no cops, specially that chavala (punk), Moreno."

It was maybe a good sign. He could maybe have called Moreno worse than a punk. Seventeen years ago Louis Lopez was born to a single mother. He was basically raised by his grandmother.

East L.A. was a turf that gangs have called home since the pachuco days of the 1930's. Mexican-Americans inherited the area known as Boyle Heights from the Russian Jews who settled there in the 1930's. East L.A. got its name because it was on the east side of the L.A. River and downtown. Circa 1938 the area around 1st and Gless was called Russian town. Many Mexicans migrated to the area during the 30's and early 40's. They labored in factories which went into overdrive during the war years. Several housing projects were built to house an influx of these workers. Gangs were formed mainly to protect turf from rival gangs from other housing projects. Some of the more notorious housing projects gave rise to the generational gangs we have today. The Pico-Aliso and Maravilla Housing Projects are still bastions of gang activity. Starting in the 1980's and unfortunately still alive and well today, gangs went capitalist and became heavily involved in the drug trade. Turf control was no longer the primary motivator. More and more youngsters were recruited, and guns became a necessary tool of the trade and an enforcer of respect.

With no father figure and not much of a family life, little Louie found himself attracted to the gang life. The O.G.'s (old gangsters) and older homies had cars, money, and women. They knew "what's up." Gang recruiters love impressionable guys like Louie because they are easy targets for gang membership. Louie soon found the acceptance and love that had eluded him by joining one of the oldest established gangs in L.A. The young pee-wees like little Louie would be the designated gun- and drug-carriers.

If they got caught, it was Eastlake Juvy for a short stay rather than county or even prison time. Many of the older homies had a tail (a police record) and would be violated and sent back to prison if caught. Louie's soul had been melted down, and he was ripe for the picking. He got a little crazy one night while strapped down with a 9mm that he was carrying for an O.G., and it earned him the Loco moniker.

Loco Louie showed up not so proudly on the following Saturday at the station ready to join the other twelve "volunteers" in our "keep L.A. beautiful program." There were two major problems, though: he was still wearing his defiant "don't fuck with me attitude" and that dopey gang belt buckle. I immediately dropped him for push-ups and he reluctantly complied. I then had him remove the belt buckle.

"How am I going to keep my dickies up, bro?"

"The title is 'officer,' not 'bro.' Give me another 25," I ordered.

Loco Louie finally started getting the message, and each week that he came to the police station to paint out graffiti, his attitude slowly improved. Don and I started adding other components to try to get these kids to see the futility of the choices they had made. The goal was to get them to start changing their own behavior. It was a fallacy to think that we could change them. Change had to come from within; they had to buy in. We were the salesmen and they were the customers. Once they bought into our rap, positive change would occur, but they had to want to change. A state parole agent I knew ran a half-way house in Van Nuys, so I asked him to bring some of his cons down to speak to the kids. A mini version of "Scared Straight" it was.

A parolee named Pedro zeroed in on Loco Louie right away.

"Bring your punk ass over here, pee-wee. You gonna be my bitch tonight. If I want, homie, you think you can take me?"

Loco knew better than to smart mouth Pedro. "No," he somberly offered up.

"Cops and cons for kids, pretty cool. I never thought I'd be on the same side as a cop in anything," Pedro said surprisingly.

Once the parolees got the kids' attention, they would sit down with them and earnestly explain the harsh realities of prison life. They would also reveal the poor choices they themselves had made in life when they were teens; choices that led them to prison. This was the stuff that gang recruiters never mentioned. Loco and the other kids listened intently and asked questions about prison rape and stabbings.

"Look it, homie," said an ex-con named Tony, who was north of six feet and solid muscle. "If I tell you to shank another homie in the joint and you don't, I'll use you, abuse you, and then take you out. The guards don't run the homeboys, we do."

The Scared Straight component definitely gave them something to think about and how tough and deadly their chosen path would be. The whole process was like squeezing ketchup from a bottle. The first few squeezes, nothing, then a few drops; you keep at it and it's Niagara Falls in red.

Louie Lopez came around. As his attitude changed, so did ours. We made him a crew chief on the neighborhood graffiti paint-outs and he liked the responsibility and respect he got from the new homies. I knew we were making progress when Louie and some of the other kids starting coming to the station, even when they weren't required to do so.

A young man who entered the program shortly after Louie was a heavy set kid name Gil Garcia. He was court-referred and hated my guts big time on his first day. I'll never forget the cop hatred that dripped like sweat from a face full of bold insolence. Gil was hard, real hard, but we jumped at the challenge. I asked Louie to help me to get to Gil, and while out painting graffiti one Saturday I heard Louie say to Gil:

"Hey, man, why you be so tough with Officer Frank? He just trying to help you, fool. I'm doing better because he really care, he helped me."

Gil listened, but was still in that "cops ain't crap" mode. Breaking their culture of hate and evil indoctrination wasn't easy, but we had to try. In a dramatic irony Louie went from a sheep to shepherd, and his help was invaluable. Most of the homies were tough enough to hang with the hard work and discipline. They would just do their time begrudgingly. The punishment angle, in and of itself, as Father Steve had advised was not going to establish the intended goal. It had to be used in the beginning to gain the respect. The dance was different with each kid, and we had to adapt. Louie helped in reading these kids and learning what made them tick. Once he learned their innermost needs, he revealed them to me, and I went to work.

I always made sure that my gun and badge were visible. It helped to intimidate and instill fear, but also gain respect. I would often tell the kids it's okay to be in a gang, but switch sides and join ours. We're down for good, not evil. Ultimately you are going to have to make that choice. It was important to get the kids to see us not as enemies. A successful way of breaking down barriers was to break bread with them. That's how Louie started coming around and opening up. I would often take them to McDonald's and buy them lunch. This provided an opportunity to listen to them in a neutral and friendly environment.

The fact that we popped for the eats didn't hurt, either. Most of these kids were hurting deeply on the inside, but they had to learn that it was no excuse for criminal behavior. If we wanted to stop the bad behavior it was important to fill that gap with something else, something positive. We held out the olive branch of having them join the LAPD Explorer Program, or becoming volunteer mentors.

It would give them purpose, as it had with Louie. When he started coming around after just a few weeks, and when I asked him to help with other homies he felt empowered. We were building him up to do good. The final bond of trust shown to him was the presentation of an LAPD cap. Since signs and symbols are important in the gang culture, the symbol of the hat went a long way. This was an indication that he and others like him had crossed the line from evil to good. We also admonished them to be careful where they wore it as it could be hazardous to their health or label them a snitch.

One day Louie showed up at the station not to paint but to talk. He was serious about leaving his gang life behind, but knew it would not be easy. I gave Louie a Bible and told him to spread the word to his homies that he was now down for God. If he got hit up with the proverbial, "Where are you from," he should show the Bible and say, "This is where I'm from." After a few weeks of this Bible routine, Louie reported that, although reluctant at first, this Bible stuff really worked.

He actually started reading the big Book and began quoting scripture even to me.

"The vineyard is full but the laborers are few," was one of his favorite quotes. This was outrageous; a hard-core homie quoting scripture to a cop!

Back to Gil who showed up one Saturday morning more hostile and pissed-off than usual:

"What's up?" I asked.

"I don't talk personal to cops, you ain't gonna be able to do nothing."

"Listen Gil, you're a good worker on the crew and I also got your back a lot more than you think. So again what's up?"

"We ain't got enough money for the rent, and me and my mom gonna get kicked out of the apartment we stay at."

"How much you need?"

"Two hundred."

I gave him a hundred and said sincerely, "Give the landlord this for now and we'll work on the rest."

"When I gotta pay it back?" he asked apprehensively.

"Forget it; we'll talk about that later."

"Thanks, Frank," he said, and the words came deep down from a place in his gut that I never heard before.

"I gotta get me a job to pay the rest."

Gil was big for his age. He wore sagging and bagging 42 inch dickies topped off with an East L.A. Pendleton buttoned at the collar. He wasn't the hiring type with this attire.

"Gil, you ain't exactly dressed for success, so we got to put you in some new threads."

I took him to K-Mart and outfitted him with a new look; regular fitted straight leg jeans and a collegiate looking sweater.

"Now that we changed your look, you are going to change your income."

Gil and I made the rounds at several local auto shops, and by the end of day he was fully employed, prepping cars at a police-friendly auto body shop.

"Riding in front don't feel right when I'm in a police ride," he said as we were driving back." I'm usually cuffed sitting in the back, not up here riding shot gun."

I threw him my cuffs and said, "Put them on if they make you feel better, and jump in the back."

We both had a good laugh.

"You ain't bad for a cop, DiPaola."

Louie kept working with Gil, even reading him scripture and talked him into coming back as a volunteer, which he did, once he finished his time. Bantering between burritos one day, Gil mentioned that he still didn't know about this God stuff. I remembered a quote from the French philosopher Blaise Pascal and told him it went something like this: "If it's a toss up whether to believe or not, and you do believe, and when you die you find that there really is a God, you win. If there isn't, it doesn't matter." With a half-hearted grin, Gil admitted he never quite thought of it that way. I eventually lost touch with him, but I'd like to think that his cop-hating days went out with his oversized dickies.

Loco Louie was now a regular visitor to the cop shop and earned the trust of most of the other officers. Since Loco Louie shared my passion for cars, I put together a detailing kit and got him a gig detailing cop's personal cars for twenty bucks a shot. Loco Louie made such a profound and complete change that even "Macho" Moreno popped for a wax job.

As a field training officer I always tried to ingrain in young cops not to get personally involved, but working with these kids it was impossible not to. Yara and I lived in the Arroyo area of Pasadena which bordered Northeast Division, but even though only a few miles away, it was really light years away. I brought Loco Louie home to spend a weekend with us and to show him that hard work and education, and taking the right path in life, could get him a fancy crib uptown.

Loco Louie's grades went up, and the homies had a "whatever" attitude towards him, now that he was down with the Lord instead of the hood rats. Loco still had some problems in the love life department when he fell hard for a classmate named Irma. Irma's father remembered the old gangster version of Loco Louie and didn't buy the epiphany routine. Things went from bad to worse when the father threatened to blow his dumb-ass head off if he didn't leave Irma alone. Loco Louie stood his ground and they almost came to blows. One night at about three in the morning Louie and Irma showed up at our doorstep. I'm thinking, "Why did I ever bring this kid to my house in the first place? Maybe I got more than I bargained for." They wanted to run away and get married.

Her old man threatened to dispose of Loco Louie by removing a certain part of his anatomy. Yara dealt with the sobbing Irma, and I was left to deal with Loco. I was in kind of a bind, because the hot tempered father had already made a runaway report on Irma, suggesting she might have been kidnapped. This was getting real heavy. Using my best interpersonal skills I went to visit the panicked papa, and personally vouched for Loco Louie.

Since she was a minor, if they got too happy with each other, Loco Louie could go to the gray bar for rape. When Irma turned eighteen they got married at one of those little chapels on Broadway, and I stood up for the newly reformed Louie Lopez. The old man never warmed up to his new son-in-law, but he didn't kill him either. Louie and Irma are still together fifteen years and three children later.

God came to Loco or maybe Loco came to God or maybe they met half way. In any event, the wayward sheep became the good shepherd who learned to love instead of hate. Once again good triumphed over evil. In a final epitaph, the new Louie became the poster boy for an LAPD recruiting poster featuring the both of us with this slogan: "Become a Cop and Help a Kid."

CENTRAL ONE

Life is tough but it's tougher when you're stupid.
— JOHN WAYNE

n LAPD-land, when things are going too well for too long, you can always figure that impending doom is just around the corner and the big one will hit. One balmy Monday morning the big one did. I rolled into the station later than usual, and Dago Don was already there sitting at his desk in our over-sized closet, euphemistically called an office in another life. It had previously housed a janitor and an assortment of mops and pails. I guess in the beginning the watch commander figured the two Dagos were all washed up, so it was appropriate. Don had his big wop cabesa nestled between two garlic-infused paws. He spent the week-end cooking a red sauce that would grace the upcoming week's worth of spaghetti.

His eyes were fixed on the fatigued desk top below as if waiting for it to respond to a question never asked.

"Who died?" I chucked off-handedly.

"We did," he responded morosely.

He raised his head and nervously rubbed a chin sporting a forlorn grimace. He spoke the foreboding words of dread that we hoped never to hear.

"Captain Carl is leaving, some mess down at Central Division where the captain there screwed up. Captain Carl is on the transfer list to un-screw it up."

Before I could let out the proverbial 'oh shit,' Don offered up some more cheerful news;

"It gets better. We're getting 'career-killer Crab' from downtown."

Captain "Career-Killer" Crab had the personality and command presence of a shoelace. He was arrogant and had a reputation for killing a lot of good cops' careers. Crab was also well-known throughout the department for his "burn 'em to learn 'em" style of lousy leadership. The cops at his prior division found him noxious at best. There were more 181's (personnel complaints) in progress than hot shots radio calls on a full moon Friday.

And just when I thought things couldn't get any worse, they did. Don and I had big-time bonded with a gangster named Shy Boy. He had plastered that moniker throughout the division and we finally made him. We both took to the kid and eventually him to us. Within a few weeks Shy Boy was ready to leave gang banging behind, and he even starred in our infamous LAPD official training video on gangs and graffiti. On one occasion we brought him back to the neighborhood he had bombed and had a local business man confront him. We filmed the business man asking Shy Boy why we had splashed graffiti all over his building.

Shy Boy responded, "I just want everybody to know that I'm standing here."

That statement prophetically said it all. He felt like somebody when we got him a job at a local car stereo shop. He even installed the speakers on my own ride. We took to him like peanut butter to jelly, and after the filming of the training tape Shy Boy proudly boasted, "I'm a star." He even fantasized about becoming a cop. A week later he was shot to death when giving the wrong answer to the perilous question, "Where are you from?" from a rival homie.

Shy Boy joined the ranks of the dishonored dead. Another L.A. gang killing that had become so numerous it didn't even make the papers. We gave a copy of the tape to his mother along with our heart felt condolences. His conversion will be forever memorialized on that film. We had built up affection and now endured the pain. The week started lousy and ended even lousier. Shy Boy's death tore at both of us like a shot in the gut. His real name was George. "Why George?" I banged my fist against that same stupid worn out piece of crap mahogany desk; the one where we first interviewed him.

"Career killer" Crab wasn't there two worthless weeks before we came to blows. First it was our "Urban Anthropology" sign that we had jokingly put up in our office that came to his attention.

"Take it down" he ordered, "Somebody will find that offensive."

We didn't, and he found that offensive and disrespectful. Captain Crab's enmity surfaced again over several recent interviews which I had given on the local TV news. I was summoned to his office for a not-so-friendly face to face.

"DiPaola, from now on, the two of you will be directly supervised by the watch commander, and no more press interviews unless you clear it through me first." He than picked up a pen and started fidgeting with it.

"Okay, captain," I responded in a matter-of-fact tone. My nonchalant attitude and response spoke volumes so he upped the ante.

"I am ordering you not only to not speak with the media, but also with any politicians or anybody of a higher rank than me." He took it a step farther and ordered me not to speak to anybody about anything. He was beginning to ramble and I cut him off.

"That's against my first amendment rights," I sarcastically threw back at him.

His nervous fidgeting increased rapidly, and he reminded me of the Captain Queeg character played by Humphrey Bogart in the movie The Caine Mutiny, when confronted by Fred McMurray. I pushed him. "Captain, there's no need to be nervous, I'm just a patrolman."

He cut me off in a rage, "Get out and report to the watch commander immediately, and from now you and your side kick will be in uniform."

I called Captain Carl with my tales of woe and two days later I was administratively transferred to Central Division. Kudos to Captain Carl.

Central Division is the smallest of all the geographical divisions, and is the home of the first LAPD police station. Thus it bears the numerical destination #1 as in "1 Adam 12," for those who remember the famed Jack Webb TV show. I was still trying to make sense of Shy Boy's senseless killing and shake the Captain Crab blues when things finally started looking up. I arrived at Central, sadly leaving Don to go it alone at Northeast. Capt Carl green-lighted the Impact Program and turned me loose. I bought a desk in the CRO office (community relations), and the CRO sergeant was told to facilitate my efforts. Captain Carl stressed to him, "You are to be a facilitator, not an administrator."

Captain Carl handed me the ball, and I ran with it. The program grew, and I received so many accolades and commendations that the entire department and even City Hall took notice. We were really making a difference in the lives of many young people. The nice thing about being a part of the CRO office was that it was also home to the Police Explorer Program, which was headed by a beefy black cop named Ramsey. Ramsey and I immediately hit it off, and when we flipped a kid who wanted to change his evil ways, Ramsey's Explorer Program filled the void. Filling the void was the key to turning these kids around, and many a young man traded in his saggin-'n-baggin' dickies for an LAPD blue Explorer uniform.

Loco was nineteen by now. He followed me to Central, where he became an official LAPD volunteer, complete with ID card and all. He was official, baby, and he loved it. Ramsey and I worked hand-in-hand. I helped him with the Explorer Program, and he helped me with Impact. Not a month would go by that we weren't headlined in the L.A. Times or a local evening news show. The publicity not only helped us, but it didn't hurt the department or Captain Carl either. One of the Explorers I immediately became fond of was a tenacious tyke named Manny Martinez. He had a happy round face and smooth wavy brown hair. The swarthy, medium-height kid had sincere eyes which provided a deep insight into his soul. He reminded me of myself when I was his age. Maybe that's why I liked him. He was good people, and that's all that mattered.

Manny grew up on Alvarado Street near the notorious MacArthur Park. He had ten siblings. Two of his brothers were ganged up and died from catching too many bullets in too many drive-by's. Gang life wasn't in his horoscope. He wanted to be a cop, and the Explorer Program was the first step to his blue glory. Manny loved cops and cops loved Manny; a rarity for a ghetto kid from the blood-stained streets of Rampart Division.

A few months and a few hundred kids later, I was approached by a producer for CBS News who wanted to do a three-part story on the Impact Program. The focus was to be on the LAPD's pro-active innovative efforts at gang intervention. He assigned Pat LaLama, that's right, the same Pat LaLama of today's TMZ fame. She was to do a headline-grabbing story that would run during their sweeps with the intended hope of boosting CBS's ratings. Not only did they sweep the sweeps, but it didn't hurt our ratings either. Pat did a bang-up job and eventually received a journalistic award. The story, however, would achieve notoriety because of a young man named Abel.

Many kids were being referred by cops, schools, and now the courts. The volume caused us to hold a group intake night for each new class. Parents were required to attend with their children. The purpose was to set the stage for the next eight weeks. This would get the kids to confront the consequences of their behavior and take ownership for their actions. Sometimes we would bring a coffin into the room or pictures of dead homies, courtesy of LAPD Homicide. The idea was to shock them and soften their attitude; most of the time it worked.

F. Scott Fitzgerald once spoke of personality being an unbroken series of successful gestures. We had to use all forms of drama, from humor and raw emotion to tenacity and terror, to keep them on the edge of their seats. They weren't there to be comfortable, and we weren't there to be manipulated or liked. I tried to pattern the program after my own military basic training experience at Fort Dix, and Police Academy training, which, if you remember, I had plenty of. The idea was to break them down, and build them back up. If it worked for the military and LAPD's raw recruits, we might have a shot with these kids.

That first intake night we were all a little nervous, especially being under the scrutiny of a popular news anchor and her camera.

"I'm here to keep you from getting killed or going to the joint. Am I your friend or am I your enemy?" This was how I began the session.

Even the hardest of the hard had to reluctantly admit I was a friend and not an enemy. It was extremely difficult for these kids to admit, especially to themselves, that the proverbial objects of their hatred, cops, could actually be friends, let alone saviors.

It was important for us to convince them of our sincerity. That's where guest speakers like Loco and other former gang members, joined by prison inmates came in. Loco had it in his DNA to do the right thing to save these kids.

"What's the matter with you fools? Don't you see that me and the cops want to help you? Your homies ain't gonna take a bullet for you, and they sure ain't gonna do your time in the pinta." Loco admonished.

I then added to Loco's repertoire, "What we're doing here today we do out of love."

One young lady yelled out: "You don't even know us. How can you say you love us?"

"One of God's most important commandments is to love your neighbor as yourself. Guess what little lady, you're my neighbor."

Now that they were softened up we went for the kill. Abel was a good looking slender sixteen-year-old who got caught up in the addictive allure of gang life. In a different time he would have been on the football team wearing a letterman sweater instead of outfitted in the gang attire of a street warrior.

Gang banging is addictive and sucks in kids who have no goals or aspirations, like quick sand. Loco and I tried to suck them out. I couldn't help but contrast the goals and experiences of my youth with theirs. In my high school the Jewish kids aspired to be doctors, lawyers, and engineers. The Italians and Irish wanted to be cops, fireman, or join the trades. Nobody aspired to be a gangster or a drug dealer. What the hell happened?

Most of the kids who crowded into the roll call room that night were Hispanic, and mostly Catholic. Some sported Christ's cross around their necks, and the evil ink symbolizing gang affiliation on their bodies. Abel was no exception with the three mi vida loca dots on the web of his hand between the thumb and forefinger. The iniquitous sign of the most dreaded street gang in L.A. was tattooed on his left fore arm. My eyes met his head on, and with my face close and menacing I fired into my rap.

"Do me a favor, cover your tattoos or remove the cross. You can't be down for Jesus and the devil at the same time. You gotta figure out who you represent, who you're down for. You can't be down both for good and evil. All you kids who are representing, and also have a cross, need to understand that Jesus and the devil don't kick it in the same crib. It offends us to look at the cross while you're representing your gang. You are going to have to decide which side of the street you're going to be down for, good or evil."

Abel was the first to cover the tattoos by rolling down his sleeve. Two of the other boys also unclenched their intestines, momentarily let go of the hate, and did the same. One defiant tough guy took off the cross and mad-dogged me. I guess we knew where he stood, didn't we? That was a major act of disrespect to God and all those present.

I told him, "So guess what, homie? You play, you pay. Get in the push-up position. This is a police station, my house, and you just dissed me. Heaven or hell? Which one?"

I needed to put these kids on the spot and get them to seriously think about the choices they were making.

Abel's story was memorialized forever that night and I still use the news clips today when giving talks on gangs. Each young man in that room had to take responsibility for his actions in front of the group and explain what led them to their criminally screwed up behavior.

"What happened, Abel? Why did you join a gang and how did you end up getting arrested?" I asked with a mixture of sincerity and command presence.

It was important to establish control and let them know that in this police setting it wasn't like school, or their house. We were in charge.

"My dad would get drunk and fight with my mom," he said sincerely. "So I would go out with my friends."

His friends were a notorious and deadly street gang. The lack of parental love and an unstable home life led him to find acceptance in a gang. This was an all-too familiar scenario played out over and over again. The traditional family unit, which in another time was responsible for instilling morals, values, and good behavior, was no longer doing its job. It was important for Abel's mother to hear that somber and sincere account from her son. She broke down and cried. The kids didn't get this way by themselves. Just as in a marriage, there are two sides to every story. This is why it was important for the parents or guardians to attend these sessions.

I eased up my approach as I asked Abel, "Do you love your mom?"

He looked down and answered, "Yes".

"Then hug her, Abel, and tell her that," I suggested.

He did, and many of the other parents clapped and cried. Even Pat and the news crew got a little misty. Intake nights usually resulted in an outpouring of emotion. Parents and kids would often spill their guts out in this most unlikely setting; the gritty, grimy, roll-call room.

In many cases we were facilitators of communication to parents and their children who were too busy, or too aggravated, to have a sincere heart-to-heart. I took to Abel immediately, but our bond was forged when I went to court with him. I spoke on his behalf about a stolen car beef he had been arrested for previously. When kids join gangs they are told that the gangs got your back. In order to take the place of a gang, we the cops, had to step up and be there for them.

Personal mentoring was vital in trying to reach the depths of their souls and penetrate the tough outer exterior. Since there weren't enough of us to go around, we had to pick and choose those youngsters that we thought we could reach. The eyes were the key to the soul, and I just hoped that I had read them right. It was that policemen's sense number six which led me to the dock of the bay. I was right with Loco, Eddie, and Shy Boy, to name a few. Operating these kids was no different than operating dope dealers. There are those I knew I could score, and others which had no vibe. Once a rapport was built and their trust earned, the shell was cracked. I could now get to the meat.

Another young man in attendance that night was a boy of light complexion and short brown hair, named Frankie Fernandez. Frankie looked like the boy next door, but in this case what you saw was not what you got. He was referred for truancy and being caught in a stolen ride.

"What kind of shoes you got on mister?" I barked.

"Nikes," he replied.

"Take them off." I made a play for them and he got sore.

"They are mine," he lashed out angrily.

"Well the car you took was somebody else's. Now you know what it feels like, don't you?"

"Whatever," was his sarcastic response.

He was dull and listless, obviously from smoking too much weed.

"How come you don't go to school?"

"Cause it's boring, and I don't need to."

"If I could prove to you that you need school would you go?"

"Maybe."

"Is Mickey Mouse a cat or a dog?"

He looked at me quizzically, and then his eyes locked on the ceiling and went blank. His wheels may have been turning but there was no traction and no answer.

"Okay, here is another one. Who did we fight in the Vietnam War?"

His cannabis-controlled mind stumbled, and then an angry annoyed response followed.

"How am I supposed to know this stuff?" he shouted back.

"Frankie, 'Life is tough, but it's tougher when you're stupid.'" This line was used famously by John Wayne in the movie, "Sands of Iwo Jima," when addressing a young Marine. The rest of the kids in the room laughed, but Frankie didn't. This kid was bathed in a blanket of arrogance and ignorance. Change came slowly, but it did come over the next eight weeks. At graduation Frankie was asked to explain how and why he changed.

"When you told me about how 'life is tougher when you're stupid it,' made me think. Since I stopped smoking weed, I'm not fuzzy no more. When I first came here I just thought 'whatever,' but you guys made me see what's up, especially Loco and Manny. So I want to say thank you, and now you guys are my friends."

Frankie had been Franked and another soul saved.

During the next several months Abel started coming around, and he asked to have his tattoos removed. Gang tattoos imprison the wearer, and mark the individual for life. We mentored Abel and became a part of his life, as we had with Loco. Somewhere along the road to recovery, Abel decided that he wanted to be a cop. Manny and some of the other Explorers who assisted in the program were probably responsible for the big blue push. Abel knew that leaving his old life behind would be risky, but he figured it was also risky being a gangster. He rolled the dice and decided to throw in with us. I found a doctor in Beverly Hills who became well known for her laser tattoo removal skills. She donated time from her busy dermatologist practice to do just that on her own dime.

I became the car pool king for Abel and several other teens who crossed over, and the ritual was established. The LAPD black-'n-white became such a regular fixture parked just off Rodeo Drive that the B.H.P.D. wanted to know what was up. After several months most of the last vestiges of Abel's old life, his tattoos, had faded into the past, albeit painfully. Going under the laser is no fun.

Abel asked if he could join the police Explorer Program, but there was one hitch. LAPD had a policy that any youngster with gang affiliation, past or present, could not join. The solution was simple. Ramsey and I filled out the app for Abel and put a resounding "no" in the "were you ever a gang member?" box. This way Abel didn't lie; we did. Abel was accepted and went to the Explorer Academy where his performance was exemplary. He left his old life behind and now he belonged to our gang. Ramsey assigned him to numerous traffic details for major events, and the former bad guy was now out there in uniform directing the good, and the not so good, citizens of L.A.

I didn't like the visibility fearing that gangster ghosts of the past would reappear and haunt him. Even though the shadow of evil had passed from Abel, the specter of danger still lurked. I guess all of us were so engrossed in the sweet smell of success that we failed to see that there was still a dark side. Abel still liked to go out with the graffiti removal crew on Saturdays and help us with the boys. He and Loco would help supervise the new impact recruits. Their presence helped, especially in persuading the pee-wees to see the stupidity of their evil ways. Who better to tell a gangster about the pitfalls of gang life than a former gangster?

Adventures in graffiti continued at Central 1. We were painting an area of run down buildings off Alameda one Saturday. I told Abel to have the boys paint everything with graffiti on both sides of the street, and then march the crew back to the vehicles. Abel came back in a sweat some twenty minutes later.

"Sir, I think you better come with me. There is a man up there who is very mad about his truck."

"What truck, Abel?"

"The truck we painted sir."

Abel and I rolled up to the hot spot and were met by an irate chap of Asian ancestry. He was starring incredulously at his newly roller painted truck. His command of the English language needed help, but I definitely got the message. Happy he was not. He initiated the encounter with the befuddled,

"The poweece paint trucks now?"

I turned on a profound PR routine, and using every word at my disposal explained that the boys were performing community service; they were so diligent in their efforts that they got carried away. The truck was pretty beat up and having only painted the cargo box, and not the cab, helped. In a stunning reversal of fortune a big smile came to his now happier face.

"I see, I see, good, good, good for boys. Is okay to paint whole truck."

I was now the one who was stunned, but if that's what he wanted we were happy to oblige. The boys played Earl Scheib, and now the cab matched the rest of the truck. He got a free paint job courtesy of LAPD, and I got out of a king-size beef. I love L.A.!!!

A dingy roll call room at a skid row police station became my tabernacle. Hundreds of kids and their parents hung from ropes with no bottoms. They looked for help and hope wherever they could find it. For better or worse, we were there with that divine dose of wisdom and reality. I felt like one of those TV preachers, except that I had a badge and gun and wasn't getting rich, at least not in the pocket book. Abel and I continued to bond and finding a common denominator helped.

Excitement to most red-blooded young boys usually comes in the form of two legs or four wheels. I always had a passion for cars and was instrumental in putting on a car show at the LAPD Academy, which brought out Jay Leno. I had Abel and several other boys assist with the show and they got a real kick out of my '69 Camaro Z-28; beef under the hood and machismo on the street. The boys could relate to a rubber burning ride in a "catch me if you can" yellow and black striped muscle car. The sounds were guttural, and its performance violent. This piece of classic iron muscle from my youth separated the men from the boys. Raw power was the Z-28's calling card, and the boys loved it. (See photo)

I not only connected with Abel and the others, but also with the vroom years of my past.

Reaching out to the community for mentors was very important, and Pat LaLama agreed to help. She organized a ride-along for Abel and some of the others on news trucks. They helped with camera equipment, and learned first hand the skills of a news reporter. The height of our media publicity came when we were showcased on an episode of ABC's 20/20. The program received national attention, and we received inquiries from communities and police departments across the country.

All of us always prided ourselves on the fact that we were doing God's work. The anonymously-written letter (see Appendix) validated that. The envelope was addressed to LAPD, Los Angeles, Calif., attention Officer DiPaola; an incomplete address and no return. L.A. is a big city and LAPD an equally big department. The fact that it reached me at all is probably a miracle. The postmark was upstate New York. Was this message heavenly sent or divinely inspired? You be the judge.

One of our most celebrated fans (as ironic as this sounds) was O.J. Simpson. He invited us to bring a busload of our kids to Long Beach to witness the filming of his movie (which was never aired) "Frogman." He spoke to the kids about choices he made growing up in a Hunters Point housing project in San Francisco. He was actually inspirational, sincere, and made a profound impression on his at-risk audience. He also invited Ramsey and me into his trailer while the youngsters were being escorted around the movie set.

We had a nice chat, and O.J. even gave us his phone number to the Bundy condominium which would later become infamous. I decided to write a thank-you letter and have Captain Carl sign it, thanking O.J. for this memorable experience. Several weeks later, after the murder of Simpson's wife, Captain Carl approached me and stated, "I know who you can get to be a mentor, and I can write him a letter also."

"Who is that?" I asked.

"Charles Manson," he responded sardonically. We both had a good laugh.

* * * * *

Markus Mayberry was a short, stocky black kid with a hoarse raspy voice. He would have been the perfect cast member for one of those black Seventies sit-coms. Momma Mayberry called me after seeing one of those news shows, because she had nowhere else to turn.

The Impact Program was unique in that we took voluntary enrollments from parents and guardians. Unlike the courts or probation you didn't have to be arrested or cited. Our goal was to reach out before it was too late. Markus was the proverbial "pain in the ass kid" who provided just the right amount of angst to make him intolerable. For a fifteen-year-old he was smart and street savvy, and knew how to run a game on someone.

I read Markus right away, and knew he would just love to get over on a cop. Confrontation would be a useless approach with him. Markus needed a reality tune up that only the cons at a local half-way house could provide. I gave them the heads up on Markus before we arrived, and they were more than willing to up the ante.

Monster Mike and Terrible Tony were waiting for the tour of terror when we arrived. Markus was the last one in line as we toured the facility, and Terrible Tony and Monster Mike brought up the rear right behind Markus. Monster Mike had a bottle of Vaseline that he kept screwing and unscrewing the cap. Terrible Tony whispered softly to Markus, "Come to prison baby and you'll be mine." The kid from hell got the message from the cons from hell. Markus ran up to me, grabbed me and said,

"This ain't no lie, Frank. Those m.f.'s want to rape me. No lie, no lie!"

Two days later I received a call from Momma Mayberry.

"What did you do to Markus, Officer Frank? He doesn't run away anymore, stays in his room and minds every word. How did you get him to do that?"

I responded, "With a little help from my friends."

ANGEL'S WAY

They sacrificed their sons and daughters to demons.
— PSALMS 106

"You don't know what's it is like growing up poor, Hispanic, and with no father in East L.A.," Myrna Martinez said defiantly.

Yara roared back at her, "My maiden name is Castellanos; I was born in Mexico, grew up in Watts, and never knew my father. And guess what, girl – I never did drugs or gang-banged so get over it and start showing some respect."

The Impact Program had always been a guy thing for bad boys. Not that there weren't plenty of ferocious females to go around but boys were hard enough to deal with. My wife didn't quite see it that way and thought we should be reaching out to girls as well. I made her a proposition. "Go to the Police Academy and become an LAPD Reserve Officer. I'll get you assigned to me, and we can include girls."

Always eager for a challenge, it was game on. At the age of 44, Yara called me on it and did just that. She was running up and down the hellacious hills of Elysian Park, mastering the penal code and close-order drill. She even put a superb spit shine to a pair of pitch black military-type shoes. Nine months later she graduated. Proudly earning the shining silver oval coveted by many, but earned only by a few.

Myrna Martinez was among our first group of girl recruits, and after that conversation with her I whispered to my wife:

"Damn, girl, right on. I think you are going to do real fine at this."

Yara displayed the badge proudly on her chest. When kids and parents focused on it, she got the respect she finally deserved; something that had eluded her as a volunteer. Myrna's attitude mirrored her personality, elusive and defiant. She melted into tears, however, after my wife's come back. She finally came around and warmed up to Yara with a hug, letting loose with a dose of sincerity from the gut and a profound, "I'm sorry."

There were six girls in the first group, and all were cholitas from the hood. Hood rats with razor thin eyebrows and lips decked out in a heavy dose of crimson, topped with enough eyeliner to fill the make-up counter at Walgreen's. One of them, named Lina, had a teased job that could have earned her a cameo role in Grease. Attitude and anger, they were all mirror images of each other at the outset, but once Myrna broke down the others softened up; just a little.

In L.A. gang culture, girls are not officially allowed to be jumped in to the male gang. They are not good enough; it's a male chauvinist pig thing. Sexism, as well as racism, is all part of the culture, if you could call it that. Girls exist primarily as sex objects and are relegated to being at the beck and call of their respective home boys. This is especially true in Hispanic gangs. The females support the males by carrying guns and drugs. Sometimes girls will form their own gang as a subset of the male gang. As with the boys, the lack of a loving, well-structured family life causes girls to seek love and protection from their male homies. Gang life is a one-stop shop for whatever is missing in their lives, or so they think.

"When you show up here on Saturday, ladies, you will have no make-up or jewelry, and you will wear the official LAPD sweats that will be issued to you," Yara barked drill-sergeant style. "You will address the men as 'sir' or 'officer' and the woman as 'ma'am' or 'officer'."

I was proud of my new militarized wife. She was soft spoken with savvy sincerity, yet had the command presence of a drill sergeant. She didn't have to yell, yet every eyeball in that soiled and discolored role call room was locked on the slender brunette with telling eyes and veracious vigor. Hope and salvation were in the offering.

"Why are you here, Lina?"

"For truancy and curfew," she lazily responded.

Lina called "Dog Town," a drug-infested neighborhood sandwiched between Lincoln Heights and Chinatown, her home.

"Why don't you go to school?" Yara asked.

"Cause it's boring, and it sucks."

"Well, that says it all, doesn't it? What are your goals and what do you want to do with your life?"

"Whatever," came an apathetic response from the diminutive Lina.

"Name one word that describes you, Lina."

"Cool."

"Why did your parents come here from Mexico in the first place?"

"For a better life, I guess."

"So why don't you stay in school, stay out of gangs and get that better life? Being 'cool' is not going to get you that better life. It's staying in school and out of trouble that's going to make your parents proud of you."

At the time I was training a black female probationary officer named Cory Cobbs. Cory jumped into the conversation and asked Lina how she spent her time.

"Kicking back," the unconcerned and inattentive young girl answered.

"I think you need to do some push-ups home girl," Officer Cobbs shot back. "Now move it!"

The in-your-face caustic commotion was necessary to establish control and get their attention and respect. Remember, in their world respect was based on fear. Confident, Cory was a natural, and I was proud to have her as a sister in blue. A black girl named Denise was chewing gum and sarcastically smiling because her cholita classmate had been humiliated by the cops. Officer Cory, all five-feet-four inches of her, leaped to the third row in a fury facing off with Denise. She opened up on her like a fifty caliber in a fox hole.

"What color am I girl?"

"Black," Denise responded.

"That's right, sista and get that gum outta your big stupid mouth."

Denise did so, and at Office Cory's command joined Lina in the push-up position. Officer Cory wasn't quite finished with her though.

"I wasn't raised in Beverly Hills, girl. I was raised in the same hood as yours. I'm in a gang too, and I'm representing."

She then took off her badge and practically shoved into Denise's now wide-opened eyes. "My gang stands for good not bad. It's us and my gang in this room tonight that's trying to save your silly ass and self-respect. Now get up off the floor, and go sit down like a lady."

After many months of mentoring madness by Yara, Cory, and other female volunteers, redemption and conversion slowly came to the once belligerent and hostile Lina and Denise. Most of the kids had the same "nowhere" attitude towards school, their elders, and life in general. They spent more time cutting classes than attending them. Many of these kids who skipped school were called housers because they would get loaded and kick back at houses when the parents were at work. Their social hip-hop and pop culture world was filled with the violent and sexually-degrading messages of gangster rap. "Bye, bye, Miss American pie" was replaced with "Bitches, ho's, bros and bullets."

I would give my Rap-Is-Crap class to expose the violent and degrading underbelly of rap and the gangster lifestyle of death that it perpetuated.

We would often ask the kids such basic questions as, "Who did we fight in the Vietnam War?" Typical answer was, "I don know." "Was Mickey Mouse a cat or a dog?" Fifty percent unbelievably got this one wrong. Yara came up with a real brain teaser with one girl named Carla. She had been referred for truancy, racking up over fifty absences. "Is the world round or flat?" Yara asked with a sarcastic smile.

The young girl smiled quizzically and her eyes headed straight to the ceiling. She hesitated for a few more seconds and then said, "flat" and shrugged her shoulders. Carla was in the tenth grade, and how she got that far is a testimony to the sad state of our school system.

"Are you sure, Carla?"

"Well it used to be flat and then became round."

Amazed Yara asked, "When did it become round?"

"When the dinosaurs died!"

These responses would have reached the height of hilarity if it wasn't so terribly telling. A lot of eyes were opened on these intake nights, and the view wasn't pretty. We had to win the battle on offense. Not by attacking the kids, but by going after their lifestyle choices. We had to get them to buy into and take ownership of their own self destructiveness.

Since parents were part of the problem, they needed to be part of the solution. Yara, along with another officer and me, instituted a series of common-sense parenting classes. They were given in both English and Spanish. Parents knew they needed help, and we gave them the necessary tools. More irony here: we did not have any kids of our own, but our classes were based on common sense, good values, and morals. Such basics as setting boundaries, having consequences, and following through, along with gang and drug awareness were presented. Communication skills were also taught. Many of these parents would just yell and never take the time to listen to their kids. They would talk at them, and not with them.

We also re-introduced parents to the importance of the dinner hour, where parental bonding over a meal could take place. This family hour provided the opportunity for family discussion and problem-solving. Parents were also advised they had the right to enter their kids' rooms unannounced to monitor for drugs and gang accessories. One would think that this would be common sense. Unfortunately parents have been reduced in their parental roles and they have bought into their lack of parental authority, deferring to an unhealthy atmosphere of too much emphasis on children's rights. Parents just don't know how to be parents anymore.

Another innovation we came up with was to take the girls to a Beverly Hills beauty salon. There they were taught the proper way of applying make-up and adopting hair styles that enhanced their appearance. It was sad that although they lived less than twenty miles away, none had ever been to Beverly Hills. Yara tried to explain to them that to achieve success, they would have to get out of that ghetto mentality, not only in behavior but in appearance as well. KCAL/Channel 9 News featured our Beverly Hills beauty visit on a news segment.

This was visionary, ground-breaking stuff for an LAPD viewed as militaristic and out of touch with the people it serves. Our approach in reaching out to the at-risk minority population went far beyond normal community policing efforts. Yara's vision and concerned, innovative style made the program far more inclusive. Many young women on the edge eventually developed into the fine young ladies they deserved to be.

With the inclusion of girls, it didn't take long for us to be playing to a full house. Once the limit was reached, new enrollees were placed on a waiting list. As in life, there are exceptions to everything, and a young girl named Lisa Lopez was one of those exceptions. She and her mother showed up at the front desk and insisted on seeing me after one of the news shows.

The typical scenario was a desperate parent with a reluctant child in toe. This one was different. With Lisa, the desperation in her eyes jumped out at me immediately when I told her the program was full. Her mother was ready to accept that, but Lisa was not. Lisa wasn't your typical cholita gang-banger. She had long black hair, an easy touch of make-up and almost no eyeliner. I was able to get right to the eyes with no gaudy distractions. They were tearful and telling. Her seventeen-year-old body was actually appropriately clothed which was a refreshing change.

Her voice sprang from her depths, "Look officer, I belong to a gang, and sooner or later I'm gonna get killed. You gotta help me. I need this program!"

My wife and I were hooked. Lisa Lopez was in. When they actually want to leave the gang life, the victory lap is in sight.

Lisa soon became one of our star pupils, easily banging out push-ups during our physical exercises and offered to help other girls who couldn't do as well. She had found the gang and drug scene very appealing in the beginning, but eventually saw the other side which was painted in pain. That wasn't for her. Lisa also got star billing in a one-hour documentary on the Impact Program which was featured on cable TV.

When she graduated she returned to mentor the new arrivals of gang wannabes and stoners. It was hope that made her see the right path, and it was hope that she gave back to the others who were in such desperate need. Upon graduating she gave me a plaque with my name on it and my name's meaning: "Frank – One of freedom. Stand fast, therefore, in the liberty with which Christ hath made us free..." (*Galatians 5:1*)

Another promising young girl was Carmen Carenza. She was named after the beautiful and talented actress and singer of the 1940's, Carmen Miranda. Her mother hoped that she too would become a singer and actress. Carmen's parents were in pocket financially due to the taqueria they poured their heart and soul into. Their daughter had it all, or did she? Material largesse couldn't compensate for family time or emotional love. Although spoiled and rebellious, Carmen started coming around.

But there was a "but." She sought lost love in a neighborhood nemesis named Juan. To her he was Don Juan, but his gangster soul belonged to the streets. She was his girl, and it cost her plenty. A bullet inscribed with Don Juan's name missed its mark but found its home in between Carmen's beautiful eyes. Carmen Miranda died peacefully in old age. Carmen Carenza died violently after a short life which ended before it even started. It was a day that many dreams died.

At the conclusion of each intake night the girls were given several questions as homework and these are some examples:

Why should I get married before I get pregnant?

What is the Golden Rule, and how does it apply to me?

What are the Ten Commandments, and how do they apply to me?

Why should I stay in school?

What are my goals and how am I going to accomplish them?

This was pretty basic stuff, but somehow the basics were no longer taught by the parents or schools. These kids were clueless as to the proper rules of behavior, and, unfortunately, but not surprisingly, so were their parents. In the 1950's, kids were mostly influenced by the following, and in this order: parents, schools, church. Today the primary influences are: parents, friends, pop-culture characters, and media. Church is a minor player, if at all, and media is a dominant influence.

This explains why today's youth know more about party dolls, salacious slick sluttish actors, rebellious rock stars, and gangster rappers, than they do about The Golden Rule, God, and country. Unfortunately, these are today's role models, who are famous for all the wrong reasons. Since proper behavior is based on morality, we had to start at the beginning. Behavior comes from attitude, and attitude comes from values. A change in values equals a change in behavior. Since most of these kids had no values and the wrong attitude, we posed the question to them, "How about putting on an attitude of gratitude?" We explained to kids and parents that if all we have is your version of truth and my version of truth, truth becomes relative. There had to be an absolute truth, and it wasn't being taught. We provided a message of salvation in a sea of sin.

THE LAST TIME I SAW ABEL

I am going to send an angel to guard you,
be attentive to him and listen to his voice.
— EXODUS 23:20-21

os Angeles Times: "The end of a life on the edge."L.A. Times
Channel 9 News: "A life lost just as it was being found…."
Channel 2 Action News: Pat LaLama - "Coming up next...a tough story
to tell you about. Seven months ago we profiled a teenager named Abel
who was turning his life around. Unfortunately, he was murdered, and
his dreams of becoming a police officer were destroyed. As journalists we rarely get
personally involved in a story, but I befriended a young man while covering a tough
gang prevention program. Abel did turn his life around, but the gang would not let
go. He was a wonderful young man with a future, but his past caught up with him.
He was stabbed to death at Topanga State Beach."

Channel 9 News: "He fought to escape the deadly grip of gangs, but Abel never
lived to see his dreams come true."

Officer Frank DiPaola, LAPD: "From one of them he became one of us…."

Officer Robert Ramsey, LAPD: "He would have been a good testament to the
community. He used to be a gang member, but now he was a success."

Channel 11 News: "The men who killed Abel are still at large…."

Abel: "I used to see my mom crying a lot but now she is happy with me…."

Channel 13 News: "L.A. police officers don't usually attend funerals of former
gang members, but when services were held inside this Hollywood church, eight
officers stood inside and wept. His mother asked that he be buried in his blue explorer
uniform, and so he was. It is how he will be remembered."

Channel 11 News: "If you have grown numb to this kind of crime, you haven't
heard the whole story…"

* * * * *

The first murder in the history of the world was a good man named Abel killed by
his evil brother Cain. Thousands of years later, and a millions of murdered souls later,
another good man named Abel was murdered. The more things change, the more

they remain the same.

Ramsey and I handled all of Abel's funeral arrangements; his parents, who spoke no English, were relieved and most appreciative. We provided a limo for the family, and CBS News popped for the flowers. It was our show and our rules. We even found a Spanish-speaking priest. Everyone was pleased except the dirty dozen, or so, devils who represented a dangerous and feared street gang. Even in death, Abel's old gang would not let go.

They dripped out of the lobby of the funeral home after Ramsey and I turned them back, one by one and out the door. They spilled on to the lawn of green; humiliated by the blue angels that confronted them. The devil's brigade had raging angry eyes and shaved heads full of hate. Encased within them were malignant minds of mayhem. We drew our 9mm's and had them prone out on the lawn. Responding uniform officers methodically searched each one. Several were booked for possessing weapons or dope. The rest were allowed to enter the funeral home only after they removed their R.I.P. (rest in peace) shirts.

When angrily asked why they couldn't wear the shirts, I defiantly told them that they represented gang attire. Abel belonged to our gang and not theirs. The shirts were also a sign of disrespect. The confrontation only added to the tension which hung as thick as hell's heat in that ghetto funeral parlor. The next day death threats poured into the station, and I even received a menacing "187" (penal code for murder) message on my pager.

Father Fabian's words were inspiring and reassuring. "Death is like reading a book, now that one chapter has ended another is just beginning."

"He who believes in Me though he dies will live forever. For some he may appear to be dead but he is only asleep." Then he quoted from Psalms, "You have given light to their eyes that they should not sleep in death."

For the believer death's finality was foiled.

Malibu, murder, and mayhem are words that usually don't go together, but on the night of October 14, 1995 they did. One reason that Abel's death received so much news attention was because gang murders don't usually occur in places like Malibu. The lush and sunny Malibu community thrives because of its escapist – almost surreal– nature. People go to places like this to escape the ghetto; on this night the ghetto came to them. Pat LaLama, of CBS News, described the tragedy most succinctly.

"What happened? Police don't know. Abel was on the beach with friends when he was confronted by several gang members. He ran from them across Pacific Coast Highway, and they gave chase. When they caught up with him there was a confrontation, and Abel was repeatedly stabbed to death."

I guess that says it all. After almost twenty years we still don't know. The L.A. County Sheriff's Department handled the investigation, but it never got any traction, and the murder today is still unsolved. Ramsey and I helped interview the group Abel was with but they weren't able to identify any suspects. We were afraid the attackers might have been his old gang because of his cop connection. We never made that tie, and we'll never really know for sure. In a previous news story on Abel having his tattoos removed, he is quoted as saying: "When somebody asks me where I'm from I'll say, 'LAPD. You got a problem with that?'"

I sincerely hoped that he didn't say that, and it was just a bravado moment for the cops and camera.

Abel's last days on planet earth were fraught with conflict. He hadn't been coming around as much, and he was starting to miss his weekly Explorers' meetings. We all have our demons, but his were playing catch-up. When Abel finally did show up to my office, he was once again wearing that stupid gang buckle which resembled the one I took away from him on that first intake night not so long ago. He gave me a dopey explanation for his absence and the belt buckle. I came down pretty hard on him and even accused him of playing us. I told him that I didn't take kindly to being sucker-punched, so if he wanted to cross back to the other side, jail or death awaited him. I angrily told him that nobody was going to make a monkey out of me, and he despondently left the station on a sour note. I didn't know how prophetic my words would be.

Abel was one of our shining stars, but I think the forces of evil eventually closed in on him again. The next time I would see the young man we all came to know and love, he was in a box.

When Abel's murder in Malibu story hit the news, juvenile division, which oversees the Explorer Program, wasn't too happy about his gang involvement. If you remember, Ramsey and I hit the big "no" in the gang involvement box on Abel's application. The day before the funeral Abel's mother called and asked if he could be buried in his explorer's uniform and he was.

We never deluded ourselves into thinking that we totally pulled Abel out of the abyss, but the struggle for this boy's soul was well fought. Heaven or hell? Righteous or rogue? We will never know if he was the victor or the vanquished. Only God knows. In the book of Psalms it is written; "His enemies shall fall before Him." Unfortunately in this tale he fell before his enemies. It is said that everything happens for a reason. He may have fought with his attackers, but in the end the fight was really within him. The truth is that when good confronts evil, sometimes suffering is the result. And as someone once said, "Life is full of hellos and goodbyes."

MANNY MARTINEZ — FROM SINNER TO SAINT

For once you were darkness but now in the Lord you are light.
— EPHESIANS 5:8

The beat up Buick Regal with the cracked windshield, and custom by crash left front fender, was your basic low-life L.A. "G" ride. Cracked windshields were standard equipment for homeboy haulers, along with broken tail lights and missing trunk lid locks. Legal police probable cause tools for curious coppers. The Buick spilled off the freeway at Manchester near LAX and headed west. The three villainous vatos (dudes) weren't headed for a plane trip, though. They were on a malevolent mission of mayhem and worse.

A journey where the wheel man was dangerously divided against himself. The driver's hands were cold and clammy. This was in direct contrast to his bewildered brow which was tense and tepid. The beams from oncoming headlights shot at him through the darkness like rogue rays from Darth Vader's death gun. Those beams paled in comparison, however, to the rays bombarding his brain. They rose from the depths of his soul, snaking their way through the layers of his gut, climaxing at a drowning brain awash in fear and confusion. Even his intestines were yelling at him; vibes of good and evil in a deadly tug of war for the soul of one Manny Martinez. The rain which had begun to fall didn't help, but only blurred the lights which converged upon him. They were like Lucifer's luminous ghosts that appeared momentarily before vanishing into the night from which they came; their purpose to taunt and terrify.

Manny accidentally crossed the double yellow several times, but that wasn't the only line he was about to cross. It was a line from good to evil which was as much a blur as the closing headlights. He was riding that rolling wreck down a road of no return. To add to the confusion, the "G" rides woofers and tweeters, which were probably worth more than the car itself, boomed a staccato of noxious noise framed in a cacophony of repulsive rap: "When da man come, can't be dumb, no hi-five just killa jive. Killa, killa, killa."

His already-troubled teenage heart was pounding louder than the killa beat. His head exploding like the jungle jive. He tried to sound strong. "You fools fucked up, man. Why didn't you fix the windshield? Now the cops have a reason to jam us!"

"We know what's up, primo, just drive and chill," shot a voice from his right, riding shotgun in the passenger seat.

Manny's demons came to him in the form of two venomous vatos; his cousin, William, (wino Willy) and Willy's carnal (brother) Pedro the Pelon. Manny was about to cross that other perilous line any moment. Anytime now it would happen. It was that dam imaginary line which separated the good from the not so good. Wino Willy gave Manny a purposeful slap on the arm and instructed him to pull over next to the building with the big liquor bottle neon.

"They should put a big dollar sign up there in big green lights, ay? Dinero for mi ruca," (money for my girlfriend) he laughed.

Pedro the Pelon was coming out of the freeze-dried mode but still dopey and disoriented from the yesca (weed) he had been blazing.

"You ready fool?" Willy asked Pelon as he turned over his left shoulder with a nervous smile.

Wino Willy than pulled his 9mm gat from his waistband and chambered a round. Pedro lethargically did the same with his. Wino Willy was the car commander and started barking orders for the stealth operation.

"Kill the lights and keep the motor running, bro, just like they do in those gangsta movies."

Like a good but reticent soldier Manny complied and drifted into a dark parking spot. The barrio bandits tumbled out and their dark souls became one with the night.

Manny was about to become the protagonist in his own Greek tragedy. He was the puppet with angels and demons pulling the strings; hundreds of little devils were poking him with pitch forks on one side and a host of angels pulling from the other side. "I could still split and leave these two stupid vatos before it's too late," he thought to himself. "Peer pressure, why did I fall for that stupid crap! Down for the familia, we gotta help each other out. Boy, what a dope I am. What the hell am I doing here?"

This whole thing started that sweat soaked night in wino Willy's crummy crib: "For the movida and the familia," his cagey cousin played the family card.

This was a friendly persuasion over too many not-so-friendly Cuervo shooters. "Help us out, primo, little cousin, help us out."

Back behind the wheel, a million thoughts were going a million miles an hour. Sweat filled his face along with agonizing angst. He was hot and sticky again, just like the night itself. Manny smelled the nasty order of his own body which filled the confines of his clothes and then lazily drifted through the Buick's cabin.

Gunshots rang out and broke the sinister silence. First one and then several; they seemed surreal. He was about to lose his stomach. An eternity passed from the time the shots rang out until the passenger door flew wildly open. Manny heard Wino

Willy's breathing before he saw him.

"Andale, fool!" he yelled as he opened the passenger door.

Pedro the Pelon threw himself into the back seat of the two door coupe. Wino Willy smashed the seat back and dove into the front next to Manny.

"Jam, primo, jam!" Wino yelled frantically.

Manny threw the selector level into the daring "D" position and full-throttled the Buick.

"This can't be happening. What if these fools wasted some sucker in there? What about Bonnie and the kids? Oh shit!" he thought to himself in a torment of fear-filled remorse.

"What happened? What happened in there?" he hesitantly asked though he really didn't want to know.

"Two black dudes came in right behind us and started talking smack for sticking up in their hood. When they eye-balled our quetas (guns) the mayate cabrones got pissed and opened up on us."

"Anybody hit?" It was a fear-filled inquiry whose response could determine his destiny.

"Yo no se, (I don't think so) my gat jammed but Pelon got all crazy and got some rounds off. The menso chino (dumb Chinese) and two hinas (girls) who were loading up on some pisto (booze) were cool and I didn't see them drop or nothing."

Now Wino Willy was wiping drops of dread from a sweat soaked cabesa.

"I dunno, I dunno. Just jam, primo, just jam."

The second of wino's jams was chorused by the yelp of a closing siren, and the battered Buick was bathed in the dreaded light of crimson strobes. The ghetto gun slingers were no longer predators but the prey. Bleached rays from narrowly aimed spotlights ricocheted off the bald head of Pedro the Pelon. Pulsating panic gripped the terrified trio. The reflection from the ominous red strobes danced eerily in the rear view mirror. As the lights closed in so did the sense of impending doom.

"Stupid fucking chino must have hit the alarm," Pelon yelled from the rear.

"Lose 'em, little primo, lose 'em!" Wino yelled in desperation.

Fear and fury gripped the Wino and the Pelon. They figured that the chase was on. They figured wrong. Manny, the reluctant renegade, was about to join an insurrection of one. Sirens screamed and filled the night time air. Danger and destiny flooded his brain like rushing water in a swollen creek.

"Should I hit the brake or the gas?" It was a question with a foregone conclusion. Manny "the wheelman" Martinez took control of that steering wheel like he should have taken control of his life. This whole road trip had his heart torn between good and evil. In the end he finally took control of his own destiny and jerked the wheel to the right. His foot found favor with the break pedal and put a stop to a diabolical destiny of death.

"Sabes que? (You know what?)" He yelled out to the barrio bandidos, and before either one could answer Manny said calmly, "Game over," his voice reeking with sorrowful resignation that it had even gone this far. As the Buick slammed to a stop Willy the Wino's temper went into melt down mode.

"Primo, you pinchi puto, what are you doing?" His bulging eyes were about to explode out of their confining sockets. More profound venom shot from evil tainted tongues as the finality of their reality sunk in.

Manny was now the principle player in his own felony car pullover. One he had seen demonstrated many times during Explorer training. This time he was on the wrong end of the drill. Manny killed the engine, threw the keys out the window, and raised his hands in a northerly direction as if reaching for heaven itself.

"This is fucked up, man!" Pelon declared.

"Why are you doing this to us? Why?"

In an authoritative voice filled with newly found command presence, Manny shot back. "Do what the cops tell you, and don't be stupid, or they will shoot your ass."

Manny was consumed with guilt and apprehensive fright about the surreal daunting daring drama erupting like a violent volcano. The battle for the heart and soul of Manny Martinez drew to a close. The angels must have bigger guns or more ammo. The final score was angels one, demons zero.

Since Manny was still a juvenile he was booked on the Welfare and Institution Code 602 WIC-211 PC (robbery). After having his Miranda rights read to him, the boy from the barrio made a full confession.

He spoke to the cops the only way he knew how; from the heart. The irony was that he could have told the cops that he didn't know that Pedro and Willy were going to rob the liquor store. He could have said they just stopped to get some cigarettes or brew. Manny had too much character and integrity to lie even if it meant saving his hapless hide. Had his voice not been so truthful he might have beaten the rap. His integrity ran deep and was Mr. Clean with the truth, the whole truth, and nothing but the truth.

Manny was transferred to Los Padrinos Juvenile Hall where he would spend five dismal days of dread. He beat himself up and precariously pondered the road of uncertain desperation that lay ahead. The assault of evil had definitely unlocked a perilous path, but at least it wasn't for eternity.

The D.A. found him unfit to be tried as a juvenile and was released pending further investigation. Manny returned to the Explorer program and confessed his sins. "To err is normal but to forgive is divine." Ramsey and I did the divine. We wrote letters on the kid's behalf urging the D.A. not to re-file the charges. During that time, Manny helped out with the Impact Program and was allowed to remain an Explorer, since technically he had not been convicted of a crime. He excelled in every aspect of the Explorer program and became an excellent role model and peer mentor. He was determined to make amends and put the past behind him.

Almost a year to the day the D.A. refiled the charges, charging Manny as an adult. We were all devastated. He was arraigned, pled guilty, and given a court date. Ramsey and I started a letter-writing campaign on his behalf. Every cop and kid at Central who knew him took to the tablet. Even Captain Carl wrote a glowing letter praising Manny's attributes and pleading his case. Captain Carl went a step further by emphasizing that Manny would make an excellent police officer some day and that a felony conviction would destroy that dream.

On the day of reckoning a half-dozen committed coppers showed up in uniform to make a statement to the court on Manny's behalf. As the six of us sat behind the defendant in the first row, we were approached by a hostile female D.A. She apparently took great umbrage to our uniform presence. She intuitively discerned that I was the ring leader and acrimoniously approached me.

"Aren't you officers on the wrong side of the room? Since when does LAPD sit with the defendant?" Her voice was wrapped in a sandwich of sarcasm and indignation. She may have been of the fairer sex, but that's the only part of her that the adjective applied to.

"When it's the right thing to do," I shot back with an equal dose of sarcasm and dead aim resolve.

She was a gladiator in a skirt. When it was my turn to speak I emphasized to the court that Manny had no record and performed his duties at Central 1 with character and integrity. I furthered emphasized that he immediately complied with the officers' commands and pulled his vehicle over. This was in defiance of what the other two robbery ring leaders told him to do. He also made a full voluntary confession.

The peoples' mouth-piece was a venomous vixen. She angrily inhaled her breath and lowered her brow. Her diabolical diatribe went something like this:

"Your honor, the defendant could have backed out at any time. He was part of a criminal conspiracy and a direct participant in the commission of a felony where a firearm was used. His co-defendants received five years in state prison. This defendant should receive the same."

The eyes of the viper met mine in a total affront to my paternal presence. I was afraid that Manny's fate was sealed. Our goose had been marinated in mock and was about to be cooked. The vicious vampire went for Manny's jugular. Any hope of her compassionate compliance was voraciously vanquished. Manny's optimism did a slow fade to a sullen sickening sadness. Our eyes met each other in desperation at what we knew was sure to follow. After a wrath-filled rebuke of Manny's diabolical deeds, the judge announced to the court the dreaded decision. The bell was about to toll for the boy from the barrio. The knock-out punch would cause a two year tumble.

"In concurrence with the District Attorney and since a firearm was used in the commission of a felony, the defendant, Manny Martinez, is sentenced to two years in the California Youth Authority. Bailiff, take the defendant into custody."

Manny's eyes hugged the ground. I sprang from my chair and belted out:

"Your honor, I…"

The judge cut me off at the knees.

"You are out of order officer, now sit down."

I stood my ground and I was going to be heard no matter what. The malevolent magistrate roared again:

"One more word from you and you will be taken into custody for contempt of court."

Manny gave me the last glance from a forlorn face as he was led to lock up. Two sets of eyes danced in dissolution. Was it the end or just the beginning? It was dark justice, and he would endure. After the crucifixion there was a resurrection. Manny Martinez would have his.

The California Youth Authority Southern Reception Center (SRC) is nestled in an area of suburban Los Angeles called Norwalk; mostly track homes and strip malls. The dictionary defines the term reception as, "the act or manner of receiving or a greeting or welcome." Euphemisms are always nice but a prison is a prison. Dens of degradation would be more precise, but I guess that wouldn't look good on a sign. The manner of receiving for Manny was bold and brash, definitely unwelcoming to say the least. This would be his purgatory for the next two years. Dorm rooms enclosed by a towering wall topped off menacingly in barbed wire trim.

Constant combat, sometimes mortal, and repeated rapes provided the perverse entertainment for the guests. That is why they call the C.Y.A. "gladiator school." Only the strong survive. Manny was able to avoid most of the mayhem by his quick wit and confident demeanor. He could be confrontational enough when he wanted to, but had enough savvy and moxie to know when to turn it on and when to turn it off.

I started visiting Manny at his new home away from home as often as I could. A bond between us was forged. He proved to be a model prisoner and his silver tongue earned him staff accompanied field trips to speak at local juvenile halls. For me the two years passed as quickly as a summer shower; however for Manny it was an eternity. The sun eventually shined and illuminated a new day; a day of freedom.

The first order of business for Manny was a job so he could support his family. Manny needed to transcend the past and reclaim the future. His self-worth also needed a tune up and a good job would provide the spark plug for the cylinder. This proved to be easier said than done. Jobs for convicted felons are as elusive as sun burns in a rainstorm. A two-year stay at Cal-State Norwalk didn't win any points in the resume department. After discouraging days of disillusionment, the coveted prize of meaningful employment seemed more elusive than ever.

Manny had nothing, but believed in everything. A lasagna lunch at Palermo's with yours truly soon led to a reversal of fortune and an end to his pessimistic plight. Singing Sal took to Manny immediately and offered him a job bussing tables. Manny jumped in with both feet and became the best busboy Palermo's ever had. He soon worked his way up to a waiter's spot. His salary and self-worth soared.

Meanwhile back at Central 1, the Impact Program began to grow, grow and grow. When he was not passing out pasta, Manny became a major league program player. He took ownership of the intake nights, preaching to a packed house of troubled teens. He wrote the word consequences big and bold on the blackboard. An arrow on each side descended to define the ultimate consequences; death or jail. The dynamic depth of emotion he generated was sensational and over powering.

"My name is MC211", he shouted to the packed roll call room. "For two years that's who I was. I was dehumanized; a number instead of a name."

He than banged on the chalkboard next to the word jail: "This was my consequence, people...jail, and it sucked. When you're in there you go crazy. Did you ever see a mouse in a cage? It just goes round and round."

Manny then pointed to the word death. "I know about this, too." His voice dropped a notch or two and made melancholy. Sorrowful resignation replaced the bellicose bellowing voice of seconds past. "My two brothers were ganged-up, and now they are both buried. Killed in drive-by's; they died for nothing. So don't look at me homies and think that this vato up here shooting his mouth off don't know what's up. I know too much about what's up, and it ain't my brothers, unfortunately. The only thing up about them was an R.I.P. mural on the back of a building in an alley full of trash. How many of you are clicked-up? Come on raise your hands?" His voice was authoritative and defiant. This was his show, his night.

One young man made the mistake of yawning. Manny sprang on him like a lion; his voice irascible and intimidating. "Do you think I'm fucking with you? I am not fucking with you. If I was a shot caller in the joint and you did that, you'd become my bitch and I'd punk you for your canteen and anything else you had. Your stupid silly ass would be mine." His sorrowful eyes of anger were met by sorrowful eyes of regret.

Manny turned from savage to savior, his voice now soft and sincere only inches from the mouth that would yawn no more. "You have no idea of the fate that awaits you, mijo (son). You have to learn how to love."

A tear then dropped from a pair of watery eyes; Manny got to the kid and the kid got it. The method was the message. "Get God and you'll get love. If you love you won't hate. Those are the steps that will keep you from the cemetery and jail. You know what else it would keep you from, boys and girls?"

A young girl with soft eyes and a scared face raised her hand. "Hell?"

"You got it, miss. What's your name cause that's the answer I was looking for?"

"Marisa."

"Give Marisa a hand."

Hands clapped. The drama paid off and Manny managed a home run. "Nobody gets out of here alive, so you're either going to go north or go south. Live by God's word, and north it is."

Hardened hearts and muddled minds. Nobody had ever talked to them this way. Another young girl made the mistake of laughing and maniac Manny lit her up.

"The only difference between you and me sweetheart is what you got between your legs, so stop disrespecting me, your mom, and most of all yourself. You bleed and you hurt, just like everybody else. So start paying attention, and you might just get it."

He then turned to the wide-eyed mother. "Mom, when was the last time you told your daughter you loved her?"

"I don't know."

"Wow, that's too bad. When was the last time you took her to church or talked to her about God and right from wrong?"

"I don't know."

"Why is she here, mom?"

"For disrespecting, and she don't listen."

"Did you ever teach her the Commandment 'Thou shall respect thy mother and thy father'?"

"No."

He then turned to the girl, "Did you know you were breaking one of God's commandments?"

"No."

"Mom, I think you need to have a long talk with your daughter and bring God into it. Death is eternal, young lady, you have a pretty face. It wasn't made to be pounded into a dirty cement floor, while your dignity and humanity is taken away from you."

The young lady laughed no more, and mother and daughter were overwhelmed in a valley of tears. Manny's voice turned tame.

"When was the last time you told your mom you loved her?"

Her face sank sad. She grabbed her mom and the two hugged emotionally. A transgression forgiven and a relationship renewed. Hopefully, it would last.

Manny had plenty of time to brush up on his biblical reading in "gladiator school." There were several favorite verses in his repertoire. One of his favorites was: "For once you were darkness but now in the Lord you are light." He tried tirelessly to get these kids out of the dead-end darkness that was engulfing their humanity and their soul. He wrote this quote from Ephesians on the board and would have them explain in their own words what it meant. He beat them up with tough talk, but in the end he lifted them with love.

The truth was in him, and the medium was the message. The cross that he carried led to the path of a new life; Manny Martinez, savior of souls. He got so good at this gig that the L.A. County Sheriffs borrowed him for their at-risk program called V.I.D.A. (Vital Intervention and Directional Alternatives), which they modeled after Impact. They would even fly him in their helicopter to in-take nights at outlying stations.

In his personal life Manny was a tenacious tiger as well. A friend of mine owned a large Chevy dealership, and I approached him about employment opportunities for Manny. Palermo's was okay, but he needed to earn more money. I explained that he had become like a son to me and considered him to be like a piece of gold. Manny was hired and started as a lot boy. He was sent to General Motors training school and within six months rose to the position of a service adviser. Today he is an assistant service manager for Mercedes Benz. He and his wife went through the R.C.I.A. (Rite of Christian Initiation of Adults) at their local parish and became full fledged Catholics. They bought a new home where they could raise their two children and got remarried in the Catholic Church as a proud affirmation of their faith. I think you can guess who his best man was. Tough times don't last, tough people do. And it's not always bad news. As it says in *Galatians (6:9)*, "So let us not grow weary in doing what is right, for we will reap at harvest time if we do not give up."

HOLLYWOOD: A SHOT AT STARDOM

The world is your oyster.

— SHAKESPEARE

ietzsche said, "To do is to be." Kant said, "To be is to do." And of course, Old Blue Eyes, Frank Sinatra said, "Do be do be do." When it came to deciding what I wanted to be and do, I got bit by two bugs. One was being a cop. And the other was being an actor.

Back in 1973, and I was in big L.A. on a big vacation. Snow and sleet left behind for sun, fun, and palm trees. The Sunset Strip was made famous in many movies, but would be forever memorialized in my teenage New York brain by the detective series "77 Sunset Strip." The show starred Efrem Zimbalist, Jr. and Roger Smith who later became Ann Margaret's husband. The heart throb of millions of teenage girls however, was the vibrant valet parking attendant Ed "Kookie" Burns.

To a kid growing up in the east coast, TV land always made California look like a young person's fantasy land; babes in bikinis, hot rods, classy convertibles, malt shops, and Malibu with Annette Funicello. California had it all and I wanted in. On vacation, I gazed at the Hollywood Hills and Sunset Boulevard below from the balcony of the Hollywood Hyatt Hotel. Down the street was the infamous 77 Sunset Strip, and I promised myself this illusory vision of adventure would eventually fold into my reality.

Upon returning back home, life in New York would never be the same. I had been bitten by the bug that screamed "California Dreamin" and was hooked. To make that dream a reality I focused on my destiny to become an L.A. cop. The second part of "California Dreamin" was to become an actor. I didn't want to be just in Hollywood, I wanted to be a part of it.

There's an old adage that says, "If you do good it comes back at you." That saying was never as true as it was in my introduction to the motion picture industry and a thespian's shot at stardom.

The steeple at St. Andrew's Church in Pasadena stood big and tall, and when it rang on this night, it rang for me. Most Catholic churches have chapters of St. Vincent de Paul where lay volunteer ministers and assist those in need. Yara and I were privileged to be two of those volunteers. Fortunately on this day it was our turn to make deliveries of food and clothing to the poor of the parish.

St. Vincent de Paul was a noble Frenchman named Monsieur Vincent before he became a priest and ultimately a saint. Although he was from a peasant family, his father knew that education was the key to success and sacrificed greatly to send him to the University of Toulouse. Soon afterward he was ordained a priest and sent to Marseilles. On returning he was captured by Barbary pirates who sold him as a slave in North Africa. Using his cunning and quick wit he eventually escaped. He was also a man of great ambition, character, and virtue. During his extraordinary life St. Vincent de Paul ministered to the wealthy as well as the poor. He eventually established ministries throughout Europe to aid the poor as far as necessities and to aid the wealthy in a spiritual manner. He did this by founding a congregation of priests who devoted themselves to the conversion of sinners. It almost sounds like the same work we were doing at Central except we weren't priests, because we were still doing God's handiwork.

As we pulled into the parish parking lot, we were approached by a bevy of movie trucks and trailers. Location managers often call on St. Andrew's Church for exterior and interior shots. I casually struck up a conversation with a couple of extras on the set. They informed me that the easiest way to break into the business and get exposure was to become an extra. They provided me with the phone number of a casting agency and I was on my way.

A week later found me on the set of the early 1990's crime drama, "Jake and the Fat Man," starring Joe Penny and William Conrad. Being an old movie buff, I was quite familiar with William Conrad, whom I had seen in countless movies playing a cop or a gangster. Now I would actually be working with him; what an honor. When the producer learned that I was a real cop, my status on the set changed. It was during the filming of a drug bust in one particular scene that lady luck called. I approached Joe Penny and informed him that real cops would never conduct a bust in that manner. Joe called the executive producer and director over. To my surprise he told them that Frank thinks we should do the scene another way. They then told me to lay out my scenario which I did. When we were ready to shoot the take Joe said:

"Frank, when the camera is on you, say whatever a real cop would say."

So when I pointed my gun at the bad guys, I told them, "Hold it! Don't move!" Not brilliant, but it was real.

"Cut, we'll print that one. Good job, Frank," the director yelled.

We shot the scene in one take, and Joe's next words floored me and made my dream come true.

"Get Frank a contract," he told the assistant director. Joe then shook my hand and offered up the following: "Congratulations! You are no longer an extra but an official actor. We'll get you a contract to join the Screen Actor's Guild."

The Catch-22 about the acting profession is that you can't get an agent or an audition if you aren't in the guild, and you can't get into the guild unless you have had a speaking part.

Joe Penny solved the dilemma. It was literally the stuff dreams are made of. Many aspiring actors spend years trying to get a speaking part in a major TV series or motion picture. I got my big break in just two days. The producers asked me to be the show's technical advisor and inquired if I could procure real LAPD cops for the scenes involving police officers instead of extras. Eventually, I became a regular on the show and was known as "Frank the cop." It all started while we were shooting a scene at the famous Sand Castle Restaurant on the beach in Malibu. Joe wrote in a scene for me where I'm sitting in the bar and Joe walks in, pats me on the shoulder, and says:

"Hey Frank, did your wife have a boy or a girl?"

"Twins, a boy and a girl."

During a shot in Long Beach I was asked to double as a real cop and help with traffic control. My prop police uniform had fictitious Costa Del Mar police patches. As I stopped traffic a befuddled motorist looked at my patch and asked:

"Costa del Mar? I thought I was in Long Beach. Where the heck is Costa del Mar?"

"You are in Long Beach, sir. This is just a movie uniform."

"If you are not a real cop, how can you direct traffic?"

"Well, I am, but today this is just my play uniform."

His mouth opened wide and gave me:

"Huh?" and drove off in massive confusion.

Welcome to La-La land, I thought to myself and chuckled.

Over the next two years of shooting the series almost half of the cops at Northeast and Central doubled as thespians on the set. A lieutenant humorously came up to me and mentioned that while he had been on vacation he watched an episode of "Jake and the Fat Man." He said he saw half the cops at the station on the tube.

"Even on vacation I can't get away from you guys," he joked.

If I were to become a serious actor I would have to secure an agent. No agent would touch me without a demo tape and a resume including professional acting classes. I enrolled in several acting workshops where I learned various techniques and the finer points of the craft. My demo tape was taken from a scene in the movie, "Glen Gary, Glen Ross." The scene I used was the one where Alec Baldwin berates and comes down hard on his fellow salesmen.

Acting is a profession that looks easier than it really is. Before I fell into the business I always said to myself, "Oh, I can do that." After all, my undercover role as Frankie Apollo was basically acting. When you have to memorize lines, play off other actors and the camera, it's a different ball game. My acting classes were invaluable and taught me a great deal about myself. The best acting is instinct; then we rely on our craft. Characterization is an aspect of ourselves; it's what we bring to the table. An actor can't rely only on personality but must focus on the intentions of the character he is playing. On a purely physical level the main points that had to be focused on were eye contact, being in the moment, and embodying the character physically. This meant getting my body into the act and letting body language come into play. The actor must be in his power keeping body and voice in sync. It was fairly easy due to my police training which served me well. Keeping one's voice in the body refers to not screaming or engaging in hysteria. An example would be one of my favorite movie idols, Humphrey Bogart. In most scenes, he was powerful, but he did it without yelling.

A truly professional actor must go through a serious exercise of intense introspection and self-examination, bearing the essence of his soul. The questions I learned to ask myself were and still are the following:

How do I see myself?

How do others see me?

Who am I really in actuality?

Acting is analytical. Dissecting a scene and figuring out the intention, then making the other person feel what I feel. I had to learn how to put myself in the state I was supposed to be in. Daisy, my drama coach, would often yell at me, "Frank, you are acting. You are not in the moment."

One of the most difficult aspects was to personalize the scene so I didn't have to think about what to do. If I was playing an angry part I had to actually get angry. The biggest mistake an actor usually makes is to become too dramatic. To avoid this, a good actor should always be in their essence. Coach Daisy had us make choices based on the following characteristics of animals.

Dog – loyal, protective, strong – not emotional

Wolf – cunning, swift, tough, and steadfast

Bear – strong

Lion – unyielding, protective, and domineering

Daisy told me that I was attached to the traits of a lion and should focus on those traits when doing a scene. I used many of these exercises to help the youngsters in the Impact Program. This would help them get in touch with themselves and who they really were. Unfortunately, their overexposure to our pop culture society emphasized emulating all too many wrong role models and assuming a flawed value system of violence and degradation.

My acting ability eventually reached the level that I was able to find representation with a well-respected talent agency in Century City. Even though many of the "Jake and the Fat Man" roles were small, being listed on my resume as a regular cast member helped me secure other roles such as on: "Bay Watch," "Unsolved Mysteries," "Melrose Place," and "N.Y.P.D. Blue." On "Melrose Place" I had several speaking parts opposite Heather Locklear who was great to work with. On the set of "N.Y.P.D. Blue" I had the pleasure of working with four great actors: Dennis Franz, Gordon Clapp, Kim Delaney, and Jimmy Smits. They were all very helpful and equally inspiring.

Most of the interior, as well as many of the exterior scenes of this New York-based drama, were actually filmed in L.A. In an episode entitled, "These Old Bones," I played a uniform cop who discovers a dead body in a garbage strewn vacant lot adjacent to a graffiti ridden building. The scene was actually filmed in a transformed lot on 6th and Wall Streets in the heart of skid row. Coincidentally, this was directly across the street from Central Police Station where I worked. Even when I was acting, I was back in the ghetto. Another episode of "N.Y.P.D Blue" entitled "The Truth is Out There" was filmed on the 20th Century Fox lot, which was also where the production office of "N.Y.P.D. Blue" was located. They really made me feel important, like a big-time actor. They provided me with a personal trailer with my name on it. When it was time for hair and make-up, they worked on me in my very own trailer. I could get used to this acting gig big time.

Acting is an excellent way for individuals to learn new communication skills and channel energy in a creative way. With the help of other actors and the Screen Actor's Guild, we put together a theater arts program as a component of Impact. Gang members from different gangs in the program acted along side each other and were forced to interact in various scenes. This facilitated communication and got them to look at each other similarly as human beings rather than rivals. They began to realize that they had more in common than that which divided them. Unfortunately, back on the street they would often revert back to the roles of prescribed gang members.

The cast of "N.Y.P.D. Blue" admired my work in the Impact Program and filmed a documentary at the police station which helped to facilitate play-acting with the kids. This segment was called "Inside N.Y.P.D. Blue." On the day of one of my appearances in a role in "N.Y.P.D. Blue," Channel 7 Eyewitness News hyped the segment with the quote, "A bit of Los Angeles in tonight's N.Y.P.D. Blue; meet the local cop who gets his shot at stardom. See it on Eyewitness News."

My biggest and most nerve-racking role came to me in a movie of the week called

"Wolf Pack," starring Dennis Weaver. I played a corrupt cop in a corrupt town holding the town's people at bay in a scene with many extras, sirens, and a lot of commotion. Here I was playing opposite Dennis Weaver, who I remembered from the long running series of long ago, "Gunsmoke."

He achieved fame as Marshall Dillon's side kick, Chester Goode. James Arness played the Marshall Dillon character. As a kid, I can remember we all wanted to be like Marshall Dillon and get the bad guys. How many Marshall Dillon's do we have as role models today?

"Wolf Pack" was filmed at the Warner Bros. Studios in Burbank. The scene started with my lines. The noisy crowd and Dennis Weaver's dialogue played off me. I went into my lines, and the director yelled from his bull horn an annoyed:

"Cut! Frank it sounds like you're reading your lines; you have to make this thing work."

The cast of thousands were looking at me along with Dennis Weaver. I approached the director and asked him if I could ad lib a little and then go into my dialogue.

"I don't care what you do, just make it work," he said impatiently.

I was extremely nervous to begin with and now had to crawl out of the humiliating funk that had overtaken me and do it fast. With renewed determination and vigor, I again went up to bat. This time it was a home run. The director yelled:

"You nailed it. Cut and print!" He gave me thumbs up.

Dennis Weaver was the consummate gentleman, shook my hand and said, "Good job."

Defeat is only temporary unless you let it conquer you. It was, and I didn't.

GOVERNOR PETE AND ME

Mankind was my business. The common welfare was my business; charity, mercy, forbearance, benevolence, were all my business. The dealings of my trade were but a drop of water in the comprehensive ocean of my business!
— CHARLES DICKENS

The best way to keep young men out of jail is to keep fathers in the home."
– Governor Pete Wilson

In his State of the State Speech in 1996, California Governor Pete Wilson said, "How can we call ourselves a civilized society when a three-year-old girl is killed in a hail of gun fire, simply because her family's station wagon took a wrong turn, on a street controlled by a gang? Gang activity is nothing less than the hijacking of our neighborhoods by urban terrorists...."How much better to prevent crime then to solve it."

And as one of the ABC News stations said, reporting on the speech, "As part of his solution to gang violence, Governor Wilson pointed to LAPD officer Frank DiPaola, who runs a program for teens in trouble in L.A."

It was a usual day with the usual routine phone calls in the CRO office at Central. One phone call which interrupted the routine wasn't so ordinary however.

"DiPaola, it's for you. It's the Governor's office on the phone."

I thought that the secretary was kidding, but she was on the level. The voice on the other end belonged to a young lady who identified herself as Lesley from the Governor's office. She was calling me on behalf of Governor Pete Wilson. The Governor had seen me on "20/20" and read an article on the Impact Program in the New York Times. The Governor was organizing a conference at the Burbank Hilton Hotel entitled "The Summit on the Fathers."

The theme was how fatherless boys contribute to criminal behavior. The Governor wanted me to be a speaker at the event and to bring one of the boys from the program. I was surprised, honored, and, of course, readily agreed. A young man named Robert Robles was chosen. He had had some minor run-ins with police, but ultimately, embraced by the light, he decided to change his ways. Upon graduating J.I.P., he became a peer mentor and Police Explorer. The pee-wees saw him as a role model. Robert was very effective with his communication skills and flipped more than a few pernicious pupils. He was also featured on a K-CAL channel 9 news clip.

The night before we were to meet with the Governor, Yara asked me if I should be preparing a speech for the big day. I have always been an off-the-cuff, bottom line guy, and Lesley hadn't been big with the specifics of the conference. She made it sound more like an informal round table affair.

Robert and I wore our freshly-pressed uniforms complemented with shoes spit-shined to the nines. Off we went. Upon our arrival at the Hilton, we found the place was packed, and there were more than a couple of news trucks in the parking lot. That should have been my first clue that we were in for more than we bargained for. We were directed to the main ballroom, which was filled with a cast of thousands with multiple news cameras. The official count put the attendance at about seven hundred.

We were greeted by Lesley, the consummate professional voice on the phone, who in person was Miss Ivy League herself. She extended a well-manicured hand of welcome, and then pointed to the stage and seats next to the Governor and several other dignitaries. I began to get that sinking feeling. It was akin to being on a boat that was about to sink and you can't remember where you put your life preserver. Robert looked at me in disbelief. His mouth was opened but nothing was coming out. I was as nervous as he was, and was wishing I had listened to Yara and prepared something. I knew what Robert was thinking and so was I. Let's get out of here before we make fools of ourselves. I told him not to worry; just be himself and speak from the heart.

"But all these people will be looking at me; I'm going to freak out."

"Just make believe they are all naked and you won't get nervous," I said with a smile.

He responded with an edgy, "okay," but I knew it wasn't.

Wilson's executive assistant, Lesley, ushered us into a small meeting room to meet the Governor before the conference began. Governor Pete Wilson was slight of build. He had a genuine hand shake and a folksy smile and manner to match. I made sure my handshake was firm and deliberate, backed up by a sincere "thank you" and strong eye contact.

Pete Wilson and his policies had always impressed me. I was even more impressed with him in person. He wasn't showy or pretentious. He appeared to be extremely genuine and likeable. The Governor enjoyed meeting Robert and Robert also thanked him for the opportunity to speak. I added that I didn't know if we were really prepared. I had been expecting a smaller more informal setting, but together we would do our best. He put us at ease and then it was show time. The Governor began the conference by explaining his purpose for the summit:

"Kids with uninvolved parents have a greater tendency toward criminality. Boys need the love, guidance, and discipline that fathers provide. Being a father means more than writing a check, and they must live up to their responsibility. We must change our culture and get back to two-parent families, since families are the pillar of civilization."

His sincerity in wanting to stem the tide of gangs really came through. This wasn't going to be just another dog and pony show. The intent of the conference was to showcase what different organizations were doing to intervene with at-risk youth. I figured I could handle my part or at least muddle through it, though I was feeling bad for Robert. I knew he was sweating it. If he could have pressed a button to disappear, I knew he would; like, "Beam me up, Scotty." The Governor then introduced me.

"Officer Frank DiPaola, of the LAPD, runs a program for troubled boys. He is here to talk about this fine program and its effectiveness in keeping boys out of jail."

It was do or die, so I did. "I'm not going to throw a lot of statistics at you. I'm just going to tell you what works and what doesn't in rehabilitating kids."

The audience gave my announcement major applause after being inundated with repetitive statistics and drawn-out monologues by some of the previous speakers. I felt that they and the Governor were ready for some straight talk, and that's what I gave them.

"Recently I received a letter from the mother of a young man named Justin. She said that I had become like a father figure and role model to her son, and that his behavior had made a profound change for the better. I was flattered, but it's pretty sad and a pathetic commentary that a cop who saw this kid only twice a week is the only positive role model in his life. His father had been "g.o.a." which is cop talk for gone on arrival. Raising a boy without a father is like a car without a steering wheel or a ship without a rudder. You put them out there and hope they end up on the right course. Most kids are not born evil or born bad, and if they are given the proper direction and a cause, the results can be amazing."

Speaking of causes, I then shot them the Abel truck graffiti story which resulted in a hardy laugh from the Governor and the crowd broke out in raucous applause.

"Police can no longer afford to be involved only in crime suppression but must also involve themselves in the root causes of criminality as well. We have to start dealing with these kids on the front end rather than just the back end. The juvenile justice system doesn't work very well. If it did we would not have the gang problem we have today. At best, it's only half effective when it's effective at all. That is why I created this program."

It was now Robert's turn and I prayed for a home run. He was introduced by the Governor, and the mic was his.

"I'm a Police Explorer at LAPD, and I'm doing my best so that I can eventually become a police officer. It helped me to change my life."

This was followed by a moment of silence and than he bowed his head. When it surfaced he looked vaguely at the crowd but his eyes were turned inward.

"This conference is about fathers (pause). I never had a father in my whole life."

His face was framed in sadness and regret for what might have been but wasn't. Tears sprang up. A heartfelt lament for a long departed dad and missed moments of a relationship that never were. Once the tears started, empathy from the crowd ruled and seven hundred souls rose up in a chorus of clapping and tears. Even the Governor was teary eyed. Robert saved the day and made more of an impression through hurt-filled human emotion than any prepared speech could have. I rescued him from the mic and moved in with the following:

"I would like to add that Robert is a valuable part of our mentoring program. Once a young man changes his ways, other kids would rather hear it from someone like Robert rather than from a guy like me. They figure what do I know. Sometimes they are right, what do I know?"

The audience and Governor laughed, and I pushed forward. Humor is an effective way to break the ice and doesn't hurt in the building of a rapport either.

"In addition, we try to instill a positive value system. On that note, I'll tell you a funny story. A young man in the program got picked up for causing a disturbance at a local restaurant. For punishment we gave him an extra fifty hours of community service. His mother thought this was a bit extreme and advised me that she was going to check with her family attorney. She later called back and stated that her attorney said it was fine with him, and the police were doing the right thing. The attorney must have been a Republican."

That comment brought down the conservative side of the house. Judging from the Governor's broad smile it earned me kudos from the Governor and his staff. I finished my repertoire by stating: "The Juvenile Impact Program was not an actual LAPD program; it was a bottom-up endeavor to reach out to kids on the edge. It was started by me with the help of some enlightened brass. I realize those two words don't always go together."

More raucous laughter followed.

Shortly after the summit I was called by the Governor. He truly wanted to know what could be done to stop gang violence. I advised him that the best way was to stop young people from joining gangs in the first place, and to give them an opportunity to exit gangs once they joined. I explained my two-pronged approach.

"We want them to be good, because they are good people. We do this by instilling positive character traits such as integrity and virtue, with an emphasis on morality and the Ten Commandments. Since the civil law is based on the moral law, this is only common sense."

I further explained that we give decision-making classes and teach youngsters the best ways to make choices. "We emphasize decision-making based on analytical thinking and morality, rather than anger, emotions, and feelings. It is amazing that so many of these kids had never been exposed to these life-building essentials. The media and its pop culture have replaced parents and churches in the instruction of the young. These kids have bought into a false culture.

"The second prong was a heavy emphasis on consequences. If they didn't want to be good because they were good people, they should be good because they are afraid to be bad, ultimately facing the consequences of death or jail. That is why the prison and morgue exposure was so important."

The Governor bought into my philosophy and visited the police station on several occasions to actually view the program. He liked our no-nonsense, in-your-face approach.

During one visit the Governor was amused by a young gang member who couldn't do any push-ups. The Governor, an ex-marine, assumed the push-up position next to the kid and added, "Even though I'm an old man, I can do more push-ups than you kid."

Everybody had a good laugh. It was soon after that that Yara and I were invited to Sacramento to be guests of the Governor at the State of the State Speech in 1996. He singled out the Juvenile Impact Program and honored us for our work.

A short time later, I was again summoned to Sacramento and offered a job by the Governor to be on his staff. He wanted me to travel to law enforcement agencies throughout California, showcase the Juvenile Impact Program, and assist those agencies with implementation for their own agency. Of course I accepted, but, not ready to leave LAPD yet, I asked the Governor if he could arrange to have me loaned to the state. The Governor readily agreed, and the state paid my salary to the city for the next two years.

"We have to come up with a title, Frank, for your new position," the Governor stated.

"How about gang czar?"

"This isn't New York, Frank, and the word czar sounds a little too communist to me," he chuckled.

His assistant suggested the title, "Juvenile Justice Liaison to the Governor." We all concurred and shook hands on it. I was even given gold seal business cards, normally reserved for his personal staff, instead of the generic blue State of California business cards.

I became the first police officer in the history of the LAPD assigned to the Governor's office and to serve at his request. One of the first departments I called on was the L.A. Sheriff's Department. I made my pitch to the captain and two deputies at the East L.A. station, and they bought in. Their program was to be called the V.I.D.A. Program, which means "life" in Spanish. Check the L.A. Sheriff's web-site today and V.I.D.A. is still serving the county well.

One of my many ports-of-call was the San Francisco Police Department. I was surprised when they, too, bought into a militaristic disciplined type of approach. A tough ex-marine patrolman named Marty Martin, of the Ingleside station, eagerly volunteered to take the program on. The captain at Ingleside asked to borrow Manny and me for their first intake night. When we showed up he prefaced the presentation with a small plea. The good captain asked Manny to soften his routine and limit the profanity.

"After all, this is San Francisco you know."

We all had a good laugh and Manny agreed to make more with the "nice-nice" and tone it down a notch. The program was successful at Ingleside and even rated a feature article in the San Francisco Chronicle during its two-year run.

We placed the program with many law-enforcement agencies throughout the state. It was a great adventure and an introduction to Politics 101.

The key to our approach was that an early intervention program had to be available to those youngsters who had not yet been arrested or cited, but were on the wrong path. The Governor had state Senator Dede Albert of San Diego sponsor legislation. He felt that having a Democrat introduce the legislation and getting bi-partisan support would insure its passage. I assisted in drafting the legislation. The bill passed and added section 601.5 to the Welfare and Institution's Code dealing with juveniles. In the juvenile justice system the two primary codes are 601WIC (status offenses such as run-a-way and truancy) and 602WIC (criminal offenses such as burglary and robbery). As I explained to the Governor and his staff, since today's 601 is tomorrow's 602, there had to be a hook for the early intervention before criminal behavior occurred.

The hook was that a parent or guardian could voluntarily enroll their child for pre-delinquent behavior, even though the minor hadn't been cited or arrested yet. If the child refused to participate, the parent or guardian could petition the court to make the child a ward of the court.

Governor Pete Wilson is a good man whose heart was in the right place. His visits to Central were not press events, and he spoke to the kids with a genuine interest in learning their motivation for criminal behavior. He also wanted to judge the program's effectiveness. During one unannounced visit, the Governor was dressed in soft clothes. This was unusual because Pete Wilson was rarely separated from his suit and tie. He and I casually walked around the police station. Upon our entering the coffee room to buy a cup of coffee from the machine, several baffled blue suitors jumped up in amazement. One even gave the Governor a salute and than reached out to shake his hand.

Pete Wilson contemplated a run for president in 1998, and his staff asked me to set up a luncheon at the L.A. Police Academy. This was to facilitate securing the backing of the L.A. Police Protective League. I did so. Unfortunately his presidential aspirations were short- lived, and never came into fruition. He is a great man who would have made a great president. I will always be appreciative of the recognition and the opportunity he gave me. Many young people throughout California were given a second chance due to his efforts and faith in our program. He truly fulfilled the obligations of his office and epitomized the notion that "He who has the power has the responsibility."

LOURDES AND THE LOVELY LADY

I don't measure a man's success by how high he climbs but how
high he bounces when he hits bottom.

- GENERAL GEORGE S. PATTON

This is something of an epilogue to my story...my story so far. It has to do with my growing understanding of the ways of the Lord. Someone once said, "If you haven't been there, no words are possible. If you have been there no words are necessary." I think most of us have been to a "there" where those thoughts have particular meaning for us. Right up there at the top of my personal list is Lourdes. Let me give you a little history on the place.

In the year of our Lord 1858, a young peasant girl named Bernadette Soubirous received a heavenly dose of the Divine. It came in the form of a vision from the Mother of God, the Virgin Mary, in the small town of Lourdes, France. What does this have to do with Manny and me? Plenty. Read on.

Between February 11th and 16th of that year in Lourdes, there were numerous reported apparitions of a beautiful Lady clothed in white, with a yellow rose on each foot. A statue of the Virgin Mary in the town square also depicted her with a rose on each foot. At the first sighting, Bernadette was with her two cousins, but only she could see the apparition which took place in a small grotto. Bernadette immediately made the sign of the cross. Fear fled her petite body, and serenity permeated her startled soul. (The visions of Lourdes were made popular in the movie, "The Song of Bernadette," starring Jennifer Jones. Those were the days when Hollywood actually made God-friendly, inspirational movies.)

There was a total of sixteen apparitions occurring at a cave-like grotto nestled in a rocky hillside. The grotto sits inside a rock-covered hill near the Gave de Pau River. The grotto was framed in wild brush-like foliage and grass that appears to be clinging to it for dear life. When Bernadette asked the Lady of magnificent beauty who she was the Lady replied, "I am the Immaculate Conception." Although a strong and devoted Catholic who attended mass almost daily, Bernadette did not know what that term meant. At first none of the town's people or the parish priest believed Bernadette. That changed, however, when she told of the Lady's explanation of who she was, that she had said, "I am the Immaculate Conception." This lent credence to her story because it was well known that Bernadette had never been exposed to that term and didn't know its meaning.

At this point a brief explanation on the Immaculate Conception is in order. According to the United States Catholic Catechism, God's plan for the mother of his Son was that she was to be conceived free from original sin. Although Jesus was conceived miraculously without Mary having had relations with a man, this is not the liturgical meaning of the Immaculate Conception. The Catholic Catechism goes on to explain that although we are all made in the image of God we still bear the onus of original sin. This is what accounts for the inner conflicts all of us face on a daily basis. Original sin is actually the opposite of God's goodness. The conflict between angels and demons, which have existed inside souls since Adam and Eve, will never end until we end. It is what it is. It is our self-centeredness, ego, and lack of humility which cause the problem. Simply put, it is giving into our desires of the flesh whether it is lust, power, gluttony, or money, etc. This all stems from the serpent (the devil) who led Adam and Eve astray in the Garden of Eden. God gave them free will and they misused it. Now we all have to live with the consequences. What I saw at Woodstock were examples of this complete and total self-indulgence. Woodstock was Adam and Eve on steroids.

During one of the apparitions, our Lady told Bernadette to ask the parish priest to build a shrine on the site of the grotto. In response to this request, the priest asked that she perform a miracle. Bernadette returned to the grotto at the appointed time, and as word spread, the priest and a large crowd followed her there. During the apparition, whom only Bernadette could see, the Virgin Mary told Bernadette to dig in the dirt with her hands and wash her face in the spring water that would appear. Bernadette dug in the dirt, but no spring water appeared.

The crowds quickly lost hope and began to mock her and to leave. Then the miraculous happened; first mud and than spring water sprang forth from the dry and dusty earth. Then more springs appeared, and they were said to have miraculous healing power at the time. Since Bernadette unleashed those springs, 166 years ago, thousands of cures and other benefits have occurred. A shrine was built at the site of the grotto as Our Lady requested. Today it is a huge Gothic Basilica, called the Rosary Basilica, which sits directly above the grotto. Thousands of pilgrims flock to Lourdes weekly. The town is actually located in the foothills of the Pyrenees Mountains on the border with Spain. Bernadette went on to become a nun, joining the order of the Sisters of Charity. She died at the age of 35 after years of suffering from tuberculosis. Her body was exhumed in 1909 and showed virtually no decay – truly a miracle. (High waters flooded through the grotto in 2013.)

I recount all of this about Lourdes because it all became very personal to me, and to Manny, and as the bond between Manny and I continued to grow and he became like a son, but definitely not a prodigal one. Unfortunately as our good relationship grew, another growth, not so good, also grew. I would often jokingly relate to Manny, "The reason I'm bonding with you is purely selfish; so that when I grow old I will have someone to wipe up my drool."

Manny came to me one day and reminded me of that statement, but than despairingly added, "Unfortunately dad, some day you might be wiping up my drool." Small lesions had deposited themselves on the brain of the boy who was now the man I loved like a son. The lesions morphed into the sometimes deadly and debilitating multiple sclerosis, or M.S. as the disease is known. It attacks the central nervous system and results in uncontrollable movements as mundane as the shaking of the hand to violent bodily spasms. Other symptoms of the disease are memory loss and numbness. With Manny it started with the uncontrollable shaking of the hand. These episodes would come and go sporadically. The disease has no cure but is treatable.

Manny injects himself every other day with Beta Serum to help control the disease and keep it from becoming worse. I thought to myself, "Hasn't this kid suffered enough?" Manny, like many of the saints, had been given another thorn in the flesh. He was on the front end of many bad blows but every time he got whacked he got up and he was stronger. It's been said that the more you suffer here, the greater the reward with be in heaven. We believe what we believe.

A poor choice had robbed him of two years of his life and the opportunity to become a cop. This disease now, if it progressed, could leave him bed ridden and even lead to an early death. He never sang the why-me song. Whenever we are together he always has a broad smile and is up-beat. Manny radiates an inner strength. He is a guy who holds strong to his convictions that the love of God will give him strength, even in times of weakness. "I will rather boast most gladly of my weakness in order that the power of Christ may dwell with me." *(2 Corinthians 12:9)*

As my faith grew so did my knowledge of the Catholic Church and its many divinely-inspired organizations, like the Knights of Columbus. (See Appendix) The multitude of saints and their intercessory powers are profound. One of these organizations is the Knights of Malta, also known as the Order of St. John of Jerusalem. Old movie buffs will remember this reference in the Humphrey Bogart's classic, "The Maltese Falcon." The order was established in 1085 as a community of monks who looked after the sick at the Hospital of St. John of Jerusalem.

In later years the Knights of Malta became a military order defending the Holy

Lands during the Crusades. In 1530, the order relocated to the Island of Malta after being ousted by the Turks in 1522. The Holy Roman Emperor Charles the V made this possible. They became known officially as the Knights of Malta and were declared a sovereign state. The Knights were highly respected by the great powers of Europe. They were ruled by a grand master who answered directly to the pope. The Order of Hospitallers was than established with John the Baptist instituted as their patron saint.

A military and religious order providing hospice care for thousands of people, the Knights of Malta have the honor and distinction of being the first order of knighthood and first order of chivalry in the Catholic Church. Most of its members were noblemen from all over Europe. The Knights have the distinction of being the smallest country in the world. In 1798, the Island of Malta was attacked by Napoleon and the Knights retreated to Sicily. In 1834, the Pope established them in Rome where they enjoy sovereignty today. Their mission is still to defend the faith and minister to the poor and sick. They now have diplomatic missions in 81 countries.

In keeping with their ministry, the Knights of Malta "hospitallers" or volunteers, finance trips for the terminally ill and disabled on yearly pilgrimages to Lourdes. These malades (sick people) are seeking divine cures for their terminal afflictions. It is through the generosity of the Knights that Manny, Yara, and I ended up as hospitaller pilgrims in Lourdes.

It all began when I approached my good friend Patrick with the Knights of Malta who was blessed with the task of screening applicants to be sponsored for the pilgrimage. The screening process is actually pretty rigid. Applicants have to be practicing Catholics and saddled with a sickness or disease for which there is no cure. These malades had to have a letter from their parish priest and attending physician. Once these requirements are met, the applications are reviewed by the hospitaller committee. A limited number are chosen. There are always more applicants than there are resources. We all hit the prayers pretty hard in the days before the review committee made their decision. The angels listened, and Manny had the winning hand.

Lourdes is the second-most visited city in France, with over five millions pilgrims annually. The malades – the pilgrims who go for a cure – are called and ride in three-wheeled carts which are either pushed or pulled by "hospitallers" or other pilgrims. Since Manny had no problem walking and didn't feel sick, he initially refused to be catered to. Instead, he wanted to cater to those who needed it. It was his humble admirable character shining through again. It was explained to him by the Knights and Dames that he was there to be served rather than to serve.

All of us who traveled to Lourdes were called to the service of others and reach new heights in our Christian life and spirituality. Bernadette is an excellent example of this type of individual in that she had a personal relationship with Christ and His Mother. This was especially true in her service to others. In society, unfortunately, sometimes those with illness or infirmities are marginalized. At Lourdes it is just the opposite. The malades are to be dignified and are sometimes referred to as kings or queens.

As Christ aptly put it, "Sometimes it is when we are weak that we realize our strength."

The relatively small city of Lourdes is always filled with visitors. I have never seen so many Catholics in one place. It was an experience for us that was even more moving than the Vatican; thousands of Catholics welcoming and being welcomed. This was reminiscent of the Virgin Mary's warm and welcoming spirit when she appeared to Bernadette. Although Bernadette was always in the company of someone else at the grotto, she was the only one who Our Lady appeared to.

At the last of Bernadette's apparitions the crowd accompanying her ballooned to several thousand, so the crowds we witnessed on this pilgrimage had a history. The throngs of people also lent a strong communal presence to what it means to be Catholic. We were never put off by the crowds. Quite the contrary they were a site to behold and swelled with an inner peace. They had a spirit of contentment and their faces were dressed in smiles as they scurried about and waited in line for the miracle baths. The processions were orderly, friendly, and reverent.

Even though the pilgrims spoke different languages and were from different countries, we never experienced behavior that was rude or crude. A spirit of love and hope prevailed.

The same essence of joy which radiated from the beautiful Virgin during the apparitions permeated the whole town and everyone in it. The flow of people who entered into the grotto area never seemed to end. This area was called the Domain. Pilgrims came with broken bodies and even damaged souls looking for peace, cures, and healing. Whether they found it or not, it was impossible for them not to be transformed spiritually.

The Divine presence is everywhere and is especially experienced when one is dipped, literally into the holy water which continually flows. We were informed that towels would not be needed because our bodies would dry instantly after exiting the baths. Miraculously, ours did, even though the outside temperature was only 50 degrees.

I figured there must have been a whole lot of divine intervention going on to create the huge Basilica they built on top of a huge rock which houses the grotto. Divine intervention is what Lourdes is all about. The hand of God, directed by his mother, is framed far more in humanity than in the surrounding geography. Although there have been fewer than a hundred confirmed miracles, this has more to do with the long and laborious liturgical process than anything else. There have been thousands of unconfirmed miracles and healings.

We had the honor of meeting one such healed soul. He was a gentleman named Jack, who was Manny's roommate at Lourdes. Several years earlier he had been diagnosed with terminal cancer. Although not a terribly religious fellow, he was sponsored for a pilgrimage to Lourdes. Upon returning home several months later, he went in for his usual chemo treatment. The doctor greeted him by telling him , "You no longer have cancer, so no further treatment is necessary."

A death sentence revoked and the miraculous occurred. With his new lease on life and faith renewed, Jack became a deacon in the Catholic Church. He is now a regular pilgrim to Lourdes.

Although he still has M.S., Manny has had only one serious episode, but unfortunately he has begun to experience numbness in his hands and color blindness. Whether or not he is a recipient of a miracle of physical healing remains to be seen, but his soul will forever be changed. He was no longer a victim of life, but a witness to it.

Lourdes is about opening our hearts to the love and grace of God and His mother, the Holy Queen of Heaven. This love of God and love of neighbor is the exit door from the cell of ego that imprisons us all. When Mary became mother of the Creator, she truly became mother of every human being.

My history and this book have been written in a divine duet. True faith gives us a sense of purpose. Many of these kids, and I, are living proof. I am often asked what happened to our society. The answer is simple; as the family goes, so goes the culture. If our families model the holy family, our "no-culture culture" might once again be resurrected. The greatest power in man is his free will, and the greatest power in God is His love and free will. We can use our free will to do good or evil. Mary's free will to do good and acceptance of Gods' will gave birth to the most important person in the history of mankind. Death and darkness replaced by hope and salvation. There are two sides to eternity. One is the human side, stressing materialism emphasized by media hype and our pop culture secular society. The other is the divine. God's way is the bottom line. One key unlocks them both. Faith is that key.

As far as this life is concerned, we are just passing through. Again, a Dickens quote comes to mind. Jacob Marley on his death bed whispers to Scrooge, "Save yourself." Scrooge looks at Marley bewildered; he doesn't get it. Okay, let me update Marley's message with a line from Carlos Santana who sang, "You've got to change your evil ways."

APPENDICES

FROM SINNERS TO SAINTS

So let us not grow weary in doing what is right, for we will reap at harvest time if we do not give up. – GALATIANS 6:9

Throughout history there have been many sinners who have become saints. Here are some I found particularly interesting:

St. Paul, the Apostle. Originally called Saul, the tax collector; he persecuted Christians until God spoke to him which caused him to see the evil of his ways and convert to Christianity. He became one of the greatest Apostles and spokesman of the Christian faith.

St. Moses. A violent gang leader who had the moniker "Cut throat." While on the lam from the law, he held up a monastery and was so inspired by the monks, he converted to Christianity and changed his life. He later died defending the monastery from thugs and pagans.

St. Olga. Olga murdered her husband's killer and others from that tribe. She became enamored by the splendor and forgiveness of Christianity and converted. She was later martyred while converting others in Russia and was put on a par with the Apostles.

St. Vladimir. Vladimir killed his half-brother in a murderous rage, and it is said that he had seven wives and over eight hundred concubines. He also built a temple to pagan gods. His desire to marry the emperor's sister caused him to be baptized as a Christian. Baptismal grace intervened and he helped spread Christianity throughout Russia and the Ukraine.

St. Camillus. Mercenary and card shark, he was a soldier of fortune heavily involved in the vices of gambling, drinking, and chasing prostitutes. His conversion began upon his father's death bed when a priest was summoned to administer the last rites. This caused a conversion, and he turned from sin to dedicating his life in helping the sick. He then formed a religious congregation for nursing the poor.

THE KNIGHTS OF COLUMBUS

The Knights of Columbus is the largest fraternal benefit order in the Catholic Church, and the world's largest lay family service organization. The Knights have 1.8 million members in 14,000 councils in over thirteen countries. The Knights take their name from Christopher Columbus, the Catholic founder of our great country. At the request of King Ferdinand and Queen Isabella of Spain, Columbus was commissioned to spread the Catholic faith.

The Knights have, as their foundation, four core principles: Charity (based on love thy neighbor as thyself), unity, fraternity, and patriotism. The Order is one of chivalry. It was started in 1882 by a young parish priest, Father Michael J. McGivney, in New Haven, Connecticut.

There was at the time a great deal of hostility toward Catholic immigrants, and dangerous working conditions prevailed in the factories that left many Catholic families fatherless.

Father McGivney established the Order to help provide for the families of the deceased Catholic men, and to promote the faith at a time when many men were joining secret societies whose views were anti-Catholic.

Father McGivney never envisioned what the Order's humble beginnings would rise to produce. During our many wars, the Knights provided recreational and service facilities to servicemen regardless of their faith. During World War I, the Order was praised by the American black community because no line of color was drawn. The Knights' motto was "Everybody welcome, everybody free."

In the 1920s, the Ku Klux Klan added an anti-Catholic campaign to their prejudices against blacks and Jews. The Knights of Columbus published books listing the contributions of blacks, Jews, and German-Americans, as well as Catholics, to counter the nativist propaganda of the time.

In the 1920s, the government of Mexico officially prohibited religious freedom and waged war on the Catholic Church. Nineteen priests and six members of the Knights of Columbus were martyred for standing up for their faith. That was almost a century ago, and it seems like so little has changed.

In 1951, the Order was successful in adding the words "under God" to the Pledge of Allegiance. Today, secularism is being pushed and morality is under attack, and the Order again is in overdrive to counter the immorality of our time.

I am a proud member of the Carmel Mission Council #4593 in Carmel, California where, along with my fellow Council brothers, we stage the Carmel Mission Car Show and Blessing of the Automobiles during Car Week on the Monterey Peninsula. The event has been successful beyond our wildest expectations, and we have been able to provide Catholic School scholarships and the bishop's seminary fund. Bishop Richard Garcia of the Diocese of Monterey presided over the blessing this year; he is a good friend and great promoter of the faith. This was an opportunity where my passion for cars came together with my faith. The annual event can be accessed online at *www.CarmelMissionClassic.org.*

A POEM FROM LAURA

Laura, 17, was a graduate of the Juvenile Impact Program.

LOOK TO JESUS

Ladies and gents and children too.
Those cranked up clowns in front of you
Demons of death have sold them a deal
They're very own lives and souls to steal
Tearing up parents and homes apart
Even stopping a young girl's heart.

The Devil's circus is now in town
Tearing dreams of cranked up clowns
With destruction Satan tries to fool you too
With tricks to steal your soul from you
But look to Jesus to set you free
He's the only hope for you and me...

— A GIRL NAMED LAURA

A LETTER FROM A PARENT

A PARENT'S HOPE

How much more can I endure? This thought never me. What has he done now? This question comes with each ring of the phone, each knock at the door. People pointing the finger at him when something goes wrong, even if he didn't do anything wrong, the blames end up on him.

Where did I go wrong?, am I to blame for his actions? I looked for answers in many different ways, support groups, prayer, well meaning friends and relatives always willing to give their advice, all the answers no solution. Hopelessness and being tired were the only feelings that I had left.

I remember when I first saw my son, so sweet, so innocent. Here I sit and wonder, What happened to my child? What will become of him will he grow up free or live his life out behind bars? Will he grow old or laid to rest in a early grave? These Questions are never far from me. I've prayed for the answers to these questions, still I get no answers.

One day I came home to find that a card that had been placed on the door by a police officer, not again, now what has he done? I cried. The message on the card told me to call and talk to this police officer. I call the number, talked to the officer, we set up a time for our first meeting. I felt, as I hung up the phone maybe there is still hope. The officer talked to us, (no one had really taken the time before). He placed my son on community service, laid down some strict ground rules, and told my son what was expected of him. The officer told us about a very important weekend that was coming up, one that should not be missed. The boys in the program (community service) will be taken to jail, to meet some men (that had served time) these men will be talking to the boys. This part of the program goes by the name **SCARED STRAIGHT**.

I watched, (held my breath), and waited for change. The change in my son was not that noticeable at first, little changes, the stealing, lying had stopped, money doesn't disappear anymore even his attitude changed (for the better). I got my son back and it feels good to hold him in my arms. It all started with a little card that had been placed on my door.

THERE IS HOPE, KEEP FIGHTING
NEVER GIVE UP

A LETTER FROM A SUPPORTER

(Notice the address. Somehow it got to me.)

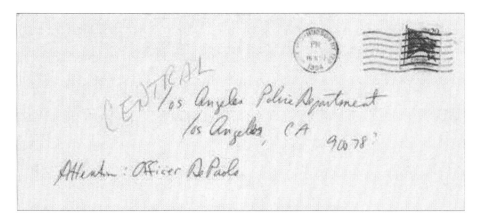

11/16/94

Dear Officer DiPaolo –

I never watch TV anymore as there is so much immorality on it. I was, however, very glad I saw "20/20" on 10/28.

I am writing to tell you that your work with the gangs and juvenile offenders is very good. You have the right idea.

May God bless you and may the Holy Spirit continue to give you wisdom.

The card is for you. Never underestimate the power of St. Michael nor doubt his existence.

Christ came to a holy Nun named Sister Faustina and instructed her to have the image you see painted. She died in Poland in 1952 and in 1991 was recognized by our Pope John Paul II.

"The two rays denote blood and water. The pale rale stands for the water which makes souls righteous. The red ray stands for the blood which is the life of souls. These two rays issued forth from the depths of my tender mercy when my agonized heart was opened by a lance on the Cross – Happy is the one who will dwell in their shelter, for the just hand of God shall not lay hold of him. – By means of this image I shall grant many graces to souls. It is to be a reminder of the demands of my mercy, because even the strongest faith is of no avail without works of mercy."

"Not in the beauty of the color, nor of the brush lies the greatness of this image, but in My grace."

God love you and protect you.

WHAT'S A COP?
(A monologue by Jack Webb from an episode of Dragnet.)

It's awkward having a policeman around the house. Friends drop in. A man with a badge answers the door. The temperature drops 20 degrees. Throw a party? That badge gets in the way. All of a sudden there isn't a straight man in the crowd. Everybody's a comedian. "Don't drink too much," somebody says, "or the man with the badge will run you in"…or, "How 's it going, Dick Tracy?" "How many jaywalkers did you pinch today?'…and there's always the one who wants to know how many apples you stole.

All at once you're lost your name. You're a "cop," a "flatfoot," a "bull," a "dick," "John Law"…you're the "fuzz," "the heat"…you're poison, you're bad news. They call you everything, but never a policeman.

It's not much of a life unless you don't mind missing a Dodger game because the hotshot phone rings, unless you like working Saturdays, Sundays and holidays at a job that doesn't pay overtime. Oh, the pay is adequate. If you count your pennies, you can put your kid through college. But you'd better plan on seeing Europe on your television set.

Then there's your first night on the beat…when you try to arrest a drunken prostitute in a Main Street bar and she rips your new uniform to shreds. You'll buy another one, out of your own pocket. You'll rub elbows with all the elite: liars, cheats, con men, the class of Skid Row and the Heartbreak; underfed kids, beaten kids, molested kids, lost kids, crying kids, homeless kids, hit-and-run kids, broken arm kids, broken leg kids, sick kids, dying kids, dead kids. The old people that nobody wants, the reliefers, the pensioners, the ones who walk the street cold and those who tried to keep warm and died in a three dollar room with an unvented gas heater. You'll walk the beat and pick up the pieces.

Do you have real adventure in your soul? You'd better have. You'll do time in a prowl car. It'll be a thrill-a-minute when you get an "unknown trouble" call and hit a back yard at two in the morning, never knowing what you'll meet…a kid with a knife…a pill-head with a gun…or two ex-cons with nothing to lose-and you'll have plenty of time to think. You'll draw duty in a "lonely car"…with nobody to talk to but your radio.

Four years in uniform and you'll have the ability, the experience and maybe the desire to be a detective. If you like to fly by the seat of your pants, this is where you belong. For every crime that's committed, you've got three million suspects to choose from. Most of the time, you'll have a few facts and a lot of hunches. You'll run down leads that dead-end on you. You'll work all-night stake-outs that could last a week. You'll do leg work until you're sure you've talked to everybody in Nevada...people who saw it happen, but really didn't...people who don't remember, those who try to forget; those who tell the truth, those who lie. You'll run to the files until your eyes ache.

And paperwork...you'll fill out a report when you're right, you'll fill out a report when you're wrong, you'll fill one out when you're not sure...you'll fill one out listing your leads, you'll fill one out when you have no leads, you'll make out a report on the reports you've made. You'll write enough words in your lifetime to stock a library. You'll learn to live with doubt, anxiety, frustration, court decisions that lend to hinder rather than help you: Dorado, Morse, Escobedo, Cahan. You'll learn to live with the district attorney, testifying in court, defense attorneys, prosecuting attorneys, judges, juries, witnesses and sometimes you won't be happy with the outcome.

But there is also this: There are thousands of men in every city who know that being a policeman is an endless, glamorless, thankless job that must be done. I know it, too, and I'm damned glad to be one of them!

BOOKS BY TONY SETON

Deki-San

Paradise Pond

The Francie Levillard Mysteries - Volumes One Through Six

Selected Writings

Jennifer

Trinidad Head

Just Imagine

The Autobiography of John Dough, Gigolo

Silver Lining

Mayhem

The Omega Crystal

Truth Be Told

The Quality Interview / Getting it Right on Both Sides of the Mic

From Terror to Triumph / the Herma Smith Curtis Story

Don't Mess with the Press /
How to Write, Produce, and Report Quality Television News

Right Car, Right Price

OTHER BOOKS FROM SETON PUBLISHING

*From Colored Town to Pebble Beach /
The Story of the Singing Sheriff* by Pat DuVal

The Early Troubles by Gerard Rose

The Boy Captain by Gerard Rose

Bless Me Father by Gerard Rose

For I Have Sinned by Gerard Rose

Red Smith in LA Noir by David Jones

The Shadow Candidate by Rich Robinson

Hustle is Heaven by Duncan Matteson

Vision for a Healthy California by Bill Monning

Three Lives of a Warrior by Phil Butler

Live Better Longer by Hugh Wilson

*Green-Lighting Your Future /
How You Can Manifest the Perfect Life* by John Koeberer

Made in the USA
San Bernardino, CA
19 June 2016